Management for Professionals

The Springer series *Management for Professionals* comprises high-level business and management books for executives. The authors are experienced business professionals and renowned professors who combine scientific background, best practice, and entrepreneurial vision to provide powerful insights into how to achieve business excellence.

More information about this series at http://www.springer.com/series/10101

Daniel Hellwig • Goran Karlic •
Arnd Huchzermeier

Build Your Own Blockchain

A Practical Guide to Distributed Ledger Technology

 Springer

Daniel Hellwig
Kepler Cannon
New York City, NY, USA

WHU-Otto Beisheim
School of Management
Vallendar, Germany

Arnd Huchzermeier
WHU-Otto Beisheim
School of Management
Vallendar, Germany

Goran Karlic
Kepler Cannon
New York City, NY, USA

.

ISSN 2192-8096   ISSN 2192-810X   (electronic)
Management for Professionals
ISBN 978-3-030-40141-2   ISBN 978-3-030-40142-9   (eBook)
https://doi.org/10.1007/978-3-030-40142-9

This Springer imprint is published by the registered company Springer Nature Switzerland AG
The registered company address is: Gewerbestrasse 11, 6330 Cham, Switzerland

Preface

Introduction to DLT: *Build Your Own Blockchain*

Blockchain technology is arguably among the most discussed innovations since the emergence of the Internet. By leveraging the concepts of decentralization, reliability, and anti-counterfeiting security, blockchain has the potential to enable a broad field of innovative applications and new forms of cooperation. At its core, blockchain brokers data in the absence of an obvious centralized authority and can help establish trust among all network participants. What's more, using blockchain technology, almost all imaginable values, rights, and obligations of tangible and intangible goods can be represented by tokens, thereby simplifying their tradability and interchange-ability. What impact this development will have worldwide remains to be seen. Cryptocurrencies like Bitcoin and Ethereum have marked the first "killer" applica-tion of this technology; however, increasing numbers of organizations are exploring how to incorporate blockchain into their existing frameworks.

Increasingly, blockchain is being recognized as an enabling protocol rather than a mere disruptive product. Naturally, this rise in prominence has been accompanied by an efflux of white papers into the public sphere that have tooted the horn of blockchain's disruptive potential; bookshelves too have been quick to fill with academically minded volumes on its theoretical and mathematical foundations. Nonetheless, despite the torrent of available material, we find that the former provides stylized and high-level discussions, while the latter opts for deeply granular and technical explanations of the technology. Neither approach equips the readers with the tools required for a practical implementation of blockchain, or with the scope of knowledge necessary for incorporating blockchain-enabled technolo-gies into existing corporate frameworks and guiding organizational decisions. As blockchain approaches its eleventh birthday, we contend that the disconnect between theory and application has lasted much too long.

Introduction to DLT: Build You Own Blockchain links theory to practice. Aimed at a non-technical audience, this book introduces each fundamental building component for understanding blockchain, followed by hands-on, problem-solving routines. Thus, in each chapter, we introduce the main ideas conceptually and practically, with subsequent chapters building on knowledge and skills acquired in previous sections. To make it as easy as possible for our readers to engage with these exercises, we leveraged Docker technology using pre-configured containers, which are the standard unit of software that packages up code and all its dependencies. This setup allows applications to run quickly and reliably from one computing environment to another and ensures that all our readers—users of Windows of macOS alike—will be able to complete the exercises with minimal technical difficulty.

The book is divided into three parts.

Part I, *Blockchain Fundamentals*, provides an overview of the main blockchain components that are relevant to practical applications and encompasses the first five chapters:

Chapter 1. Build Your Own Blockchain
Chapter 2. Conduct Your Own Transaction
Chapter 3. Choose Your Own Consensus
Chapter 4. Launch Your Own Smart Contract
Chapter 5. Deanonymize Your Own Blockchain

Part II, *Cryptography Foundations*, provides an in-depth introduction into the underlying technology foundations of the concepts explored in Part I, primarily as they pertain to cryptography frameworks and mechanisms:

Chapter 6. Encrypt Your Own Messages
Chapter 7. Provide Your Own (Digital) Signatures

Part III, *Real-World Applications*, provides a summary of past and ongoing real use cases, categorized by industry, the rationale for their choice of blockchain technology flavor, as well as the challenges faced in each instance.

Like most nascent technologies, blockchain has not been immune to the traditional hype-disillusionment-enlightenment cycle. The global market today is arguably still ahead of the technology, leading many to question the alleged significance and potential of blockchain in light of the grand promises made and the current paucity of successful and impactful implementations. However, as we continue to gain new insights into this new technology, and as more tangible applications emerge in the marketplace (e.g., money movement via JP Morgan's JPM Coin and advanced privacy controls enabled via zero-knowledge proofs), blockchain has begun to ascend the slope of enlightenment. This book aims to equip its readers with the skills necessary to harness this technology's full potential as it unfolds. As such, we hope that our readers can walk away from this book with a foundational understanding of blockchain's key implementation components, the practical knowledge required for incorporating blockchain-enabled modules into existing and future business frameworks, and valuable insights into its potential impact on economies and global financial structures.

New York City, USA/Vallendar, Germany   Daniel Hellwig
New York City, USA   Goran Karlic
Vallendar, Germany   Arnd Huchzermeier

Acknowledgements

This book was largely inspired by two courses we taught at WHU's Otto Beisheim School of Management (*Introduction to Blockchain and Blockchain Programming*) that aimed at explaining in depth the fundamental building blocks of blockchain, its ecosystem, and smart contract functionality. Although the courses are still in their prime, having taken place only in the past two years, our students have been an invaluable resource in shaping the theoretical contents and programming assignments of the course, and by extension, of the book. We have learned much from their feedback, for which we are thankful, and have sought to incorporate their dos and don'ts to the greatest extent possible.

We thank Max Mäckler and Farhan Javed for their editorial comments and extend our deepest gratitude to Dr. Jasmin Imran Alsous (Princeton, MIT) for providing detailed and substantial feedback on several drafts of this book. We are also grateful to Sonny Ajmani at Kepler Cannon for his support of this endeavor, which has been invaluable for the completion of this project.

Finally, we are delighted that Springer has given us the opportunity to work on this project. Blockchains and their potential role in our current and future societies are a topic that is sure to elicit any spectator's reaction; therefore, we hope that this book can equip our readers with the theoretical and practical know-how required to harness the technology's potential and to shape its role in our society in a meaningful way.

Contents

Part I
Blockchain Fundamentals

Blockchain Foundations

1

1.1 Introduction

A blockchain is a ledger of blocks of information (e.g., transactions, agreements) that are stored sequentially across a network of computers. Rather than a simple algorithm, blockchain is a technology construct and an enabling protocol that facilitates a decentralized brokering of data among participants; that is, its revolutionary properties do not derive from what blockchains do (i.e., store data securely), but from the manner in which they are used and implemented (i.e., trustless and decentralized). Just as the Transmission Control Protocol and Internet Protocol (TCP-IP), invented in the 1970s at DARPA [1], enabled the decentralized exchange of information (i.e., the Internet), blockchains enable the decentralized control of the transfer of assets. Indeed, the innovation with blockchain does not derive from a fundamentally new technology approach, but from the application of well-established methods of information technology (e.g., cryptographic hashing, asymmetric encryption, and peer-to-peer network architecture) to the problem of information transfer.

Blockchains enable the creation of a digital account book (the "ledger") and the sharing of data through a network of independent parties ("nodes") that are connected via the underlying internet infrastructure (Fig. 1.1). Each node has an exact copy of the ledger at every time point, thereby ensuring the creation of permanent, time-stamped transaction records consisting of the underlying blockchain nodes. Furthermore, for a record to be altered, a large part of a blockchain's network participants must simultaneously agree to change the information, and several additional safeguards must be bypassed: Once a node stores information in the blockchain database, it is next to impossible to remove it.

This chapter introduces the relevant terminology and basic functions of blockchain that predispose it to such operations, using Bitcoin as a working example.

© Springer Nature Switzerland AG 2020   3
D. Hellwig et al., *Build Your Own Blockchain*, Management for Professionals,
https://doi.org/10.1007/978-3-030-40142-9_1

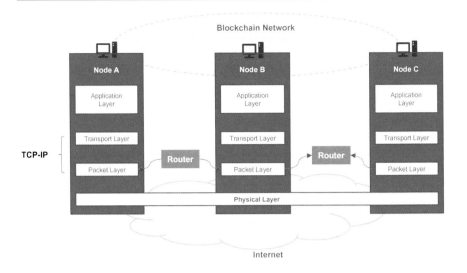

Fig. 1.1 Overview of the blockchain network infrastructure

1.1.1 Terminology

Let us start by differentiating between *blockchain* and *distributed ledger technology* (*DLT*).

Blockchain describes the data structure that stores a permanent history of transactions, while Distributed Ledger Technology (DLT), denotes a data structure that resides across multiple computing devices and is generally spread across locations or regions.

Thus, *Blockchain* is a subset of DLT and is most commonly known as the technology behind Bitcoin, Ethereum, and other cryptocurrencies. The term *blockchain* is sometimes also used to refer to the transactions and other data that are summarized in blocks and appended to a chain of already verified blocks.

"Bitcoin," the first and most widely used cryptocurrency, describes the network, the software, and the community, while "bitcoin" is the currency itself (i.e., a unit).

"Token" is a digital representation of an asset. Therefore, Bitcoins are not tokens, as they represent value themselves (i.e., as per their de facto limited supply).

"Fiat Currency" refers to a currency with no intrinsic value. Such a currency is usually established as money by government regulation (e.g., the USD or EUR).

1.1.2 The First Use Case

The Bitcoin cryptocurrency was the first blockchain application designed to enable a secure, digital, and decentralized transfer of cash between two individuals. The blockchain-based Bitcoin network provides a way of value transfer that does not rely on any external parties (e.g., banks, credit card providers). Using bitcoins, merchants can accept payments from anywhere in the world without being subject to the technical or legal restrictions that are often imposed by the existing payments infrastructure today (e.g., exchange rates, settlement delays, regulatory limitations).

However, when bitcoins are transferred, the receiver must convert them back into a fiat currency in order to be able to exchange them for other goods, unless another merchant happens to accept bitcoins as well. Since blockchains can monitor transactions that are represented in digital data, the applications that blockchains are best suited for are trustless asset transfers (e.g., cryptocurrencies). In fact, trustless asset transfers became possible only when blockchains were used to replace traditional means (e.g., bills, stocks) with digital tokens.

Cryptocurrencies (e.g., Bitcoin) are only one of many possible applications that can use the blockchain infrastructure (Fig. 1.2). Indeed, the realm of blockchain applications is vast and extends beyond the primary use case of value transfers by means of individually tracked tokens: Any real-world asset can be tracked on a blockchain, given that the underlying network functions as a mediator.

Such applications include infallible data management and identity-tracking, as blockchains can produce an exact timeline that can show who has stored what data and when. Access to such a timeline opens a multitude of options for applications across both the public (e.g., trustless land registries) and the private (e.g., cross-border money transfers) sectors.

More generally, since blockchains provide a data system that is not owned by anyone, that are free for anyone to participate in, and that are set up via a pay-to-play mechanism (i.e., there is a cost to add data), the technology is well-suited to situations in which information needs to be trusted across a network, that is, in the absence of an obvious centralized authority to broker the data in question.

As such, the main difference between traditional centralized systems like those used by banks and decentralized blockchain systems is that the former relies on a central intermediary. For example, for a traditional bank wire transfer to occur, a clearinghouse is tasked with netting out the transactions [2] that banks make between each other (Fig. 1.3). Blockchains do not need such an intermediary, as senders and receivers conduct transactions directly with each other.

Next, we review the functions and characteristics of our traditional monetary system and currencies; using Bitcoin as an example, we will then clarify the mechanisms that underlie cryptocurrencies and the blockchain technology.

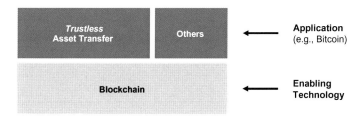

Fig. 1.2 Blockchain is a protocol-like enabling technology

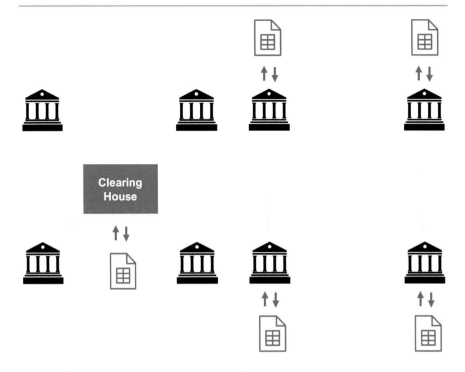

Fig. 1.3 Blockchain and the concept of decentralization

1.1.3   Currencies: Traditional and Crypto

Traditional money, like banknotes and coins, must fulfill three functions [3]:

- Serve as a *medium of exchange* to facilitate transactions.
- *Store value* (i.e., hold its value over time).
- Contain a *unit of account* (i.e., a measure to use for value accounting or comparison).

To meet these requirements, money must exhibit the following characteristics:

- *Duplication resistance*, such that it is impervious to duplication.
- *Physical security*, such that physical possession defines its ownership.

Our traditional monetary system refers to fiat currencies, that is, currencies that are intrinsically worthless objects (e.g., coins, bills) and derive their value almost entirely from their government backing [4]. Such a setup has both advantages and disadvantages: If the government that backs a currency is stable, the currency tends to be stable as well, and there are mechanisms that are in place to address trends like inflation. However, governments have failed in the past, and they will continue to do so. In such situations, currencies have historically lost substantial parts of their value, the most recent example being Venezuela.

Cryptocurrencies like Bitcoin address both the functional requirements (medium of exchange, storage of value, and unit of account) and the security characteristics (resistance to duplication and physical security) that are implemented in our traditional fiat money system.

Bitcoin, for example, allows for the direct, hidden transfer of tokens from one individual to another, thereby functioning as a *medium of exchange* by default without relying on a centralized middleman. In practice, each such transaction must include an address of origin, a destination address, and the number of tokens to be transferred. Chapter 3 provides a detailed overview of all the data elements that a Bitcoin transaction includes.

As for *storage of value*, Bitcoin most closely resembles commodity resources like silver and gold, which have a specific price per unit. Market forces (i.e., supply and demand) determine the price of these commodities, as they do the price of Bitcoin. Therefore, Bitcoin performs the storage of value requirement based on its current market-determined valuation. As such, Bitcoin is immune to most factors that would cause a traditional fiat currency to decline in value (e.g., government failure).

Finally, like traditional currencies, Bitcoin has a *unit of account*. The currency unit of the Bitcoin network is the "bitcoin," which uses the abbreviation BTC. The smallest unit is a Satoshi, named after the pseudonym Satoshi Nakamoto, the anonymous inventor of the Bitcoin network protocol (see Chap. 3). One bitcoin equals 100,000,000 Satoshis.

1.1.4   Ownership

Blockchain-based systems do not operate by sending transactions individually; instead, the nodes in the network perform transactions in so-called blocks and then append these blocks to a decentralized ledger (i.e., the blockchain). If a user owns bitcoins, the ledger shows how many coins the user has in her account (i.e., Bitcoin address) at any time. The user can transfer bitcoins to another user only if she owns them in the first place. A valid transaction instruction will update the ledger accordingly (Fig. 1.4).

As a simple example, assume that adding up all the traditional coins and bills that an individual has determines his current net worth: If I hold dollar bills in my pocket, then, for all intents and purposes, I own these dollars, and there is no ambiguity with regard to ownership.

In traditional bank accounts, large-scale databases are deployed to keep track of the amount of money that an individual has in such accounts with an institution. We can look at these systems as a centralized, continually updated ledger that tracks the amount of money each account holder has.

With Bitcoin, the system works differently. Rather than having one centralized party that controls one big ledger, every participant (node) of the blockchain network maintains one cryptographically verified copy of the latest decentralized

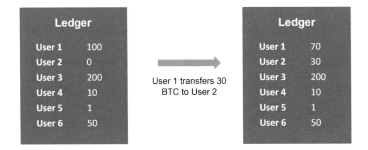

Fig. 1.4 Asset transfers via blockchain-based ledger entries (illustrative)

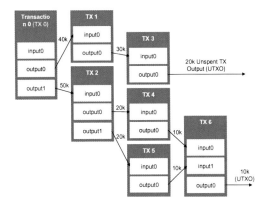

- **Input:** Every referenced input must be valid and not yet spent.

- **Signature:** Every transaction must have a signature that matches the owner of the input.

- **Inputs >= Output:** Total value of inputs must equal or exceed the total value of the outputs.

- **Unspent transaction output (UTXO):** A user's "balance" in the system is the total value of the set of UTXO coins for which the user has a private key.

- **Structure:** Each UTXO is stored with: Address, TXID and Value.

Fig. 1.5 Historic transactions determine the value associated with a bitcoin address

ledger that contains all transactions that have ever taken place. This ledger is public, so all transactions are freely accessible by anyone who is running the corresponding client software application. In fact, with public cryptocurrencies like Bitcoin, anyone can view all of the transactions that have ever taken place, although it is not easy to determine who executed the transactions. (See Chap. 5 for a detailed explanation of blockchain-related privacy and anonymity.) As of this writing, the Bitcoin blockchain has exceeded 200 GB, enough storage for roughly 50,000 MP3 songs. Each node must store the entirety of these 200 GB locally to be part of the network.

With Bitcoin, there are no account balances in the traditional sense; instead, all previous transactions that point to an address make up the value associated with this address at any point in time (Fig. 1.5). The rules for the various operations (e.g., value transfers) are determined and enforced by the software that runs on the computer nodes, which collectively form the Bitcoin network.

1.2 Cryptocurrencies

1.2.1 Control Mechanisms

In the previous section, we compared the cryptocurrency Bitcoin to its fiat money (i.e., real-world) counterpart by considering how Bitcoin's characteristics enable it to perform the critical functions of traditional money while meeting the key security requirements.

Just as in real-world fiat currencies, cryptocurrencies require processes that control the currency supply and curtail fraudulent activities. For fiat currencies, state-run organizations (e.g., central banks) manage monetary policy to control the money supply, and the state-run currency's minting/printing processes include anti-counterfeiting features (e.g., watermarks in most major bills), raising barriers to counterfeiters. Ultimately, law enforcement addresses unauthorized attempts to manipulate currency and commit fraud. In the digital realm, the equivalent of counterfeiting is double-spending, where mutually inconsistent statements (i.e., transaction messages) are made to multiple people [5], with the goal of spending the same bitcoin multiple times (see Chap. 2).

In this section, we will consider Bitcoin's operational processes in more detail and show how the characteristics of the protocol and the P2P network architecture function together to enable the Bitcoin ecosystem to perform its operations securely.

1.2.2 Cryptography

Cryptocurrencies rely on cryptography to implement security measures. Cryptography provides a mathematically based mechanism that encodes rules into the system's operations. Bitcoin, for example, relies on a handful of well-known cryptographic principles. While the underlying mathematics are simple, the encryption achieved is unbreakable within a finite time using the technical means available today [6]. The remainder of this section focuses on introducing cryptographic hashes, asymmetric encryption, and digital signatures; Chap. 8 covers more advanced cryptographic schemes, such as elliptic curve cryptography and zero-knowledge proofs.

1.2.3 Cryptographic Hashing

The oldest blockchain predates Bitcoin by thirteen years. It had been hiding in plain sight, printed weekly in the classified section of the *New York Times*. In 1991 Stuart Haber and Scott Storiette envisioned using Blockchain technology to timestamp digital documents to verify their authenticity. As part of their work with a company called Surety, the duo started to publish an alphanumeric code with weekly hash

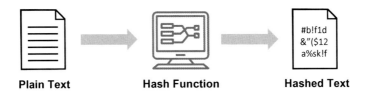

Fig. 1.6 One-way function of a hashing algorithm

summaries (for information time stamping) in the classified section of The New York Times, making the analog Surety ledger not only the first, but also the oldest blockchain in the world [7].

There are many ways to timestamp a document. Practical examples outside the digital realm include the process of sending the document in a sealed envelope with a government postage stamp and taking a picture of both the page of a document and the cover page of a major newspaper.

Similarly, within the digital realm, to provide a reliable mechanism for timestamping of digital documents, the hashing process is used to create a digital snapshot of data in time.

Cryptographic hashing, which has been around for more than thirty years, relies on non-decipherable one-way functions (Fig. 1.6). A hash function transforms data of any size into a bit string of fixed length [8]. In a nutshell, two documents (or files) can be assumed to be identical if the hashes derived from each file are identical. Therefore, publishing a hash of a document allows people to establish proof that a certain document existed at a certain point in time without sharing the actual document (i.e., because of the one-way, non- decipherable nature of the hash function). In the case of the Bitcoin network, this bit string is usually thirty-two characters long.

Bitcoin uses a hashing scheme called the Secure Hash Algorithm (SHA), which is only one of the multiple cryptographic hash functions used by the various blockchains in operation today. (See Chap. 8)

1.2.4 Asymmetric Cryptography

Asymmetric cryptography uses a pair of keys—one public and one private—instead of a single key (password). To communicate securely using this method, the recipient of an encrypted message generates both a public and a private key on his computer. The public key is used to encrypt a message that can be decrypted only by using the corresponding private key. After the recipient shares his public key with the world, anyone who wants to send him a secure message can use the public key for encryption, but only the recipient can read the message, as he is the only person who has the corresponding private key [9]. In the case of Bitcoin, the owner of an address uses the corresponding private key to authorize transactions. Chapter 8 provides more details about asymmetric cryptography.

1.2.5 Digital Signatures

A digital signature is an asymmetric cryptosystem in which a sender uses a secret signature key (i.e., the private key described in Sect. 1.2.4) to calculate a value for a digital message. Thus, using a private key, a sender can both decrypt a message after it was encrypted using his public key and sign a transaction message that allows the public to verify the authenticity of any non-encrypted message using their public key.

1.3 Network Architecture Basics

Invented in 2008, Bitcoin is an example of a global decentralized payment network with a distributed and publicly owned infrastructure, operating as a "permission-less" system. This system relies on a network architecture known as a peer-to-peer (P2P) network (see Fig. 1.7).

There is a persuasive case for Bitcoin's being the first "killer" application of decentralized computing, as one can send and receive bitcoins anywhere in the world using a P2P network, eliminating the need for a trusted third party like a bank.

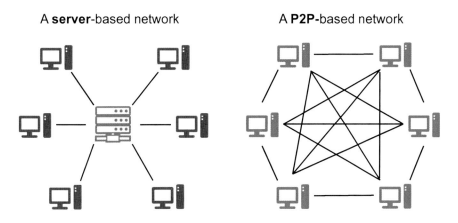

Fig. 1.7 Server-based versus P2P-based network

Permissionless blockchains are public and open for anyone to join, without barriers for entry. Since such networks can reasonably expect all kind of agents, including malicious actors, the key to secure operations lies in incenting protocol-conforming behavior in a critical majority of the network, such that:

- Malicious actors cannot take over the network through a privilege-escalation attack.
- Malicious actors cannot cooperate to launch an organized-majority attack.
- The costs of attacking the network are prohibitively high.
- The payoffs from securing the network are higher than the costs.

1.4 The Blockchain

The first three sections of this chapter compared cryptocurrencies to real-world fiat money and provided an overview of the key mechanism that cryptocurrencies deploy to perform fiat-money-like functions. Like most things, blockchains come in several flavors, but to understand what distinguishes one blockchain from another, a brief overview of blockchain's workings is in order. We will first review the operational processes of the blockchain network, as well as the individual blocks and their contents. We'll then delve into how these various elements integrate and function collectively.

1.4.1 Operations

The term *blockchain* refers to a subset of a broader category called DLTs, and derives its name from its primary activity, namely, the chronological linking of individual blocks in a chain (Fig. 1.8).

A critical feature of blockchain technology is timestamping. Every transaction and every block includes a timestamp that allows anyone to derive the correct order of all blocks since the blockchain was launched. The combination of timestamping and cryptographic hashing keeps the records contained in the blockchain unchanged. This immutability applies to every transaction and block, all the way back to the first block in a blockchain, usually referred to as the Genesis block.

1.4.2 Blocks

An individual block consists of a series of transactions that are grouped and appended to the blockchain as one unit (i.e., as a block). In the case of Bitcoin, the nodes perform the task of appending transaction blocks, a process also referred to as mining, by bundling and validating transactions that have not yet been confirmed by the network.

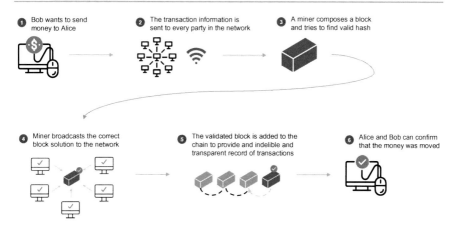

Fig. 1.8 Operational principles of a blockchain

Each block contains a set number of transactions. In the case of Bitcoin, the lowest transaction size is 83 bytes, which would allow for approximately 10,000 transactions per block. A regular transaction (i.e., party A to party B) is on the order of 250 bytes, which results in about 4,000 transactions. The number of transactions that can be included with a single block depends on the size limit of a block. As of 2019, the size limit for a block of Bitcoin was two megabytes. Note that a block contains more information than just the transaction data (see Fig. 1.9), including elements like date stamps and other reference data.

For the Proof-of-Work (PoW) mechanism deployed by the Bitcoin network, nodes must solve a cryptographic task, in addition to the bundling and validation, before they can add a new block. The process of solving this puzzle requires significant computing power, so Bitcoin is often considered wasteful in terms of its energy use, but it is the energy expenditure the network incurs that directly creates the Bitcoin value by making it extremely difficult to fake transactions. (See Chap. 3 for a closer look at the various consensus mechanisms.)

A blockchain comprises a sequence of chronologically ordered blocks that consist of transaction records that are immutable, digitally signed, and formally verified by the network nodes via the mining process.

In the case of Bitcoin, transaction records formalize the transfer of bitcoins between individual addresses. Transaction records may involve other types of information, such as property records or even more complex conditional logic in the case of smart contracts, which are hosted on a separate blockchain system, not the Bitcoin implementation. Smart contracts in the blockchain realm may allow self-triggered execution of transactions on fulfillment of pre-defined criteria. (See Chap. 5)

The smallest part of the blockchain record is a transaction, an authorized request to modify data on a blockchain, such as to send bitcoins from one address to

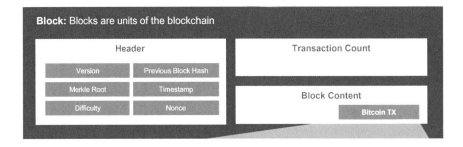

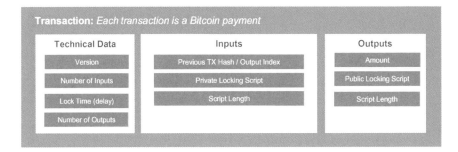

Fig. 1.9 Anatomy of a block

another. Authorization by the sender is provided using a private key, allowing all other nodes use the public key of the authorizing party to verify that signature.

All transaction requests with proper authorization (i.e., where the private key signature verifies against the authorizing party's public key) are bundled together to form the block content. The nodes take all the data that from the content of a block and capture it in a unique number, the Merkle root hash [10], which links the block content with the block header. Similarly, using all the data in the blockchain's previous block, the miners derive another unique number, the hash of the block that came before in its entirety; the previous block hash links the latest block found in the blockchain with this block.

Overall, then, the Merkle root hash, the previous block hash, a timestamp (taken from calendar time), the version and difficulty specification (both specified by the blockchain protocol), and the nonce (defined below) make up the block header of this yet-to-be-completed block (Fig. 1.9). The block remains unconfirmed until most of the network nodes validate it following successful mining by one of the network participants.

To mine and, thus, complete the block, a miner must find the correct nonce, a number that, together with the block data, will result in a unique derived number, the block hash, that fulfills the difficulty requirement (i.e., the number of zeros the uniquely derived number must contain at the end). Chapter 2 re-introduces the concept of the nonce in more detail.

As an illustration: Can you guess which integer to multiply with 123 such that the resulting number ends with 99? One option is $13 \times 123 = 1,599$, and another is $813 \times 123 = 99,999$. Here, 123 is the block data, 99 is the difficulty requirement, 13 or 813 is the nonce, and 1,599 or 99,999 represents the block hash.

The energy-intensive part of the mining is the process of finding a nonce that will result in an acceptable hash. (See Sect. 1.5.2. for more details on the immense energy requirements for confirming blocks in the Bitcoin network.)

1.5   Data Integrity

The main advantage of blockchain-based network systems is the relative immutability of their stored data entries, an attribute that makes blockchain-based solutions attractive for applications in finance and accounting, asset ownership records, and identity management that involves multiple parties. This section provides an initial overview of the critical elements of blockchain's data-integrity validation apparatus. As part of this section, we briefly introduce the concepts of ledger propagation and Merkle trees.

1.5.1   Ledger Propagation

Decentralized networks that are based on the P2P approach are generally considered more secure and more resilient than their server-based centralized counterparts are because, in contrast to networks that are based on a central server, they do not have a single point of failure. With P2P networks, malicious actors can compromise individual computers but never the entire network at once.

The introduction of the TCP/IP protocol enabled real-time transactions of information, but blockchains enable real-time P2P transactions of value. The blockchain data structure replicates across a network of nodes using a consensus mechanism that facilitates secure transfers of value between participants (Fig. 1.10). A key feature of this setup is that it allows participants to execute transactions without needing a transfer intermediary like those used by large banks.

1.5.2   Transaction Validation

In the case of PoW, the amount of time and energy required to recalculate the nonce for this block and each subsequent block is prohibitive. If a rogue actor attempts to

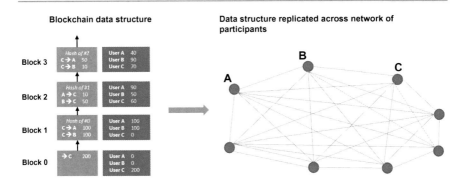

Fig. 1.10 Transfer of ledger information across the network

modify a transaction in an existing block without updating all the subsequent blocks, the mathematical validity of the blockchain breaks. (See Sect. 1.4 for more details.) In that case, all participating nodes could immediately re-validate the various hashes used in the blocks, thereby quickly determining that something is amiss.

To provide better intuition about the magnitude of energy used, consider the overall energy consumption of the Bitcoin network. As of 2018, the entire Bitcoin network computing capacity produced about 30 million trillion SHA-256 hashes per second, and the network requires approximately ten minutes to find a new hash (i.e., mine the next block). Based on expert estimates, the power consumption for the servers that run the Bitcoin software is a minimum of 2.55 GW (gigawatts), which amounts to energy consumption of 22 TWh (terawatt-hours) per year, almost the same amount of energy that the whole of Ireland uses annually.

The participating nodes of the blockchain network, the miners, perform this validation and hashing work following pre-defined rules. A computer application implements these rules, and each node that is part of the network must run this application (e.g., like the Napster software that each user had to run to exchange music files).

Consider the following example: Fig. 1.11 shows the original blocks and the transactions for Block 11. The Merkle root for the transactions in Block 11 is Hash #ABCD, which is the combined hash for the four transactions in this block. Now say someone comes in and attempts to change Transaction A to Transaction A'. Such a change modifies the hashes that the miner included previously in the Merkle tree, and the Merkle root changes to Hash #A'BCD. The hash of the previous block stored in Block 12 must now also be modified to reflect the overall change in the hash for Block 11.

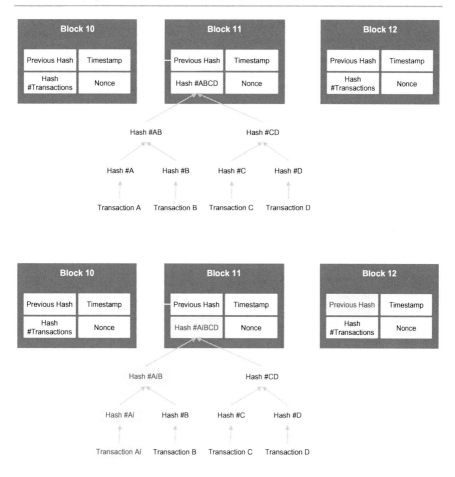

Fig. 1.11 Security through Merkle trees and hashing

1.5.3   Merkle Trees

Merkle trees, also known as binary hash trees, are tree-like data structures. Merkle trees capture the hashes of individual data items in large datasets to increase the efficiency of the verification of these datasets. Within the Blockchain realm, Merkle trees function as a tempering prevention mechanism, ensuring that no actor can secretly alter any data. The name comes from Ralph Merkel, their inventor (in 1979), and the underlying branch-like appearance of the data [11], as depicted in Fig. 1.11. For cryptocurrencies, Merkle trees help to summarize the individual transactions in each block by producing a digital transaction fingerprint. This method provides an efficient means of determining whether the network already includes a transaction in each block or not.

Blockchains are often described as immutable, but immutability implies that the data cannot be changed. The data in blockchains can, in theory, be changed, but it is very difficult to do so, as it requires the cooperation of more than 50% of the network nodes. Such attempts do not go undetected. If a malicious actor attempts a change, the other network participants can easily detect it since all operations are visible to everyone who is part of the network. The challenge for anyone who seeks to alter the transaction data stored on a blockchain arises from the fact that each block cryptographically links to the previous block. In addition to this link, each block also includes the Merkle root hash, which covers every transaction that the last block encapsulated. Therefore, if any changes occur to a transaction in the previous block, regardless of how minor, then the hash of the so-called Merkle root would change entirely along with the previous block's overall hash. As a result, each subsequent block would have to be re-calculated, given that one of the inputs (the Merkle tree hash) will have changed.

1.6 Types of Blockchains

All blockchain systems are similar in their inner workings and required functionality but differ in the way new network participants (nodes) join a network:

- Public (permissionless)
- Private (permissioned)
- Consortium-controlled (permissioned)

1.6.1 Public Blockchains

As their name indicates, public blockchains are public, so anyone can join them from anywhere. This contrasts with permissioned systems, where access to all the network access points is individually controlled (Fig. 1.12). Furthermore, new participants are unvetted, and there are no measures anyone can take to exclude a node from the network at any time. No one is responsible, and anyone can participate in reading, writing, and verifying the blockchain. Another property of this type of blockchain is that it is open and transparent. Each node in the network can review any entry from any time. The most prominent examples of public blockchains today are the Bitcoin and Ethereum networks.

1.6.2 Private Blockchains

Private blockchains require explicit pre-verification of all network nodes. Given that there is a central point of control, there is a common notion that private blockchains

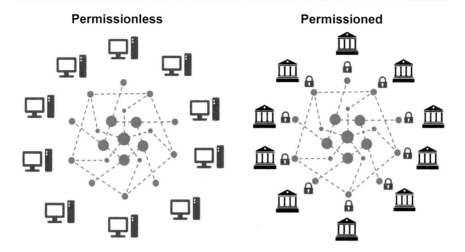

Fig. 1.12 Permissionless versus permissioned blockchains

are inferior to public (permissionless) blockchains because they have a single point of failure. Since all participating parties that run nodes in these blockchains are usually known to each other, trust is not a central concern, limiting the use cases for private blockchains. Enterprises that are particularly concerned with data privacy and control, rather than technical design, tend to use private blockchains, the most prominent of which are Ripple and Hyperledger.

1.6.3 Consortium-Controlled Blockchains

Consortium-controlled blockchains are an extension of the private blockchain setup, as they remove the centralized autonomy that is prevalent in the case of private blockchains.

For example, a consortium could consist of thirty financial institutions—or any number—which specify that decisions made in the network are accepted as valid only if more than half (16) of the participating institutions confirm it. In that sense, more than one person or company is responsible for the network. The most prominent example of a consortium-operated blockchain today is Corda by R3.

1.6.4 Selection Framework

There is no common framework that determines what type of blockchain to use in each scenario. Instead, the proposed application should drive the decision based on stakeholders' requirements. For example, most enterprise use cases involve extensive vetting before parties agree to do business with each other. As a result, consortium-operated blockchains have been prominent in early proof-of-concept (POC) implementations.

1.7 Exercise

1.7.1 Introduction

Readers will benefit from gaining first-hand experience in setting up a blockchain-based network system, as well as executing operations in this network. To that end, we have prepared a series of practical exercises for our readers to complete for each chapter in this book. Our goals are to provide the reader with the opportunity to interact with blockchain-based technology in a hands-on manner and to use a live environment to illustrate some of the concepts introduced in each of the foundational chapters.

Note that the exercises are not meant to teach coding skills or any form of implementation capabilities. Instead, we want to familiarize the reader with the working procedures of a blockchain environment. Therefore, the exercises are meant to be followed, rather than figured out.

1.7.2 Environment Setup

All exercises in the book require a Debian-like command prompt environment. To simplify the setup process, we provide a step-by-step guide to set up this environment for both Windows and macOS computers. To streamline the set-up process and minimize technical difficulties, we leverage a Linux ("Ubuntu") docker image for the exercises that we configure from scratch. (See Fig. 1.13.)

As a first step, you will need to install the latest version of Docker Desktop on your computer (macOS or Windows). For this, visit www.docker.com, create an account, and download and install the latest version of the application.

Fig. 1.13 Environment setup

Once this installation process is complete, open the console in your system to start and interact with Docker:

- In Windows, you can start the *Command Prompt* using the *Run* window. A quick way to launch the *Run* window is to press the *Windows + R* keys on your keyboard. Then, type *cmd* and press Enter or click OK.
- For macOS, either open your *Applications* folder, then open *Utilities* and double-click on *Terminal*, or press *Command + spacebar* to launch *Spotlight* and type *Terminal*, then double-click the search result. You will see a small window with a white background open on your desktop.

After you have opened the command line in Windows or macOS, use the following command in the console to download and start an interactive version of Ubuntu to run the exercises in this chapter, as well as in all subsequent chapters:

```
docker run -i -t --name pow ubuntu
```

Following this entry, you will see the following starting point, which means that you are in the command-line environment of a simulated Unix environment. You are now simulating a separate computer on your machine for the purpose of these exercises. At this point, you are ready to start the blockchain experiments. (Note that the string following the "root@" will be different than that shown in the example below.)

```
root@d708bf8dc45d:/#
```

1.7.3 Build Your Own Blockchain

With the Debian environment up and running, we can launch the blockchain environment. This environment is the prerequisite that you will need to execute all future exercises and tests. You are setting-up a local blockchain; however, this local blockchain will behave exactly like the public Ethereum blockchain that is being maintained by thousands of nodes around the globe.

(a) **Make a new directory**

Type the following commands in the command line to change to your home directory (cd), make a new directory (*mkdir*) called test1, and change into this directory. You can call the directory anything (i.e., instead of *test1*), but make sure you remain consistent throughout the rest of the exercise.

```
cd
mkdir test1
mkdir test1/geth
cd test1
```

(b) Tool download

In the command line, enter the following command to download the package lists from the repositories and update them. This list contains the most important Linux tools; an updated list is required for this as well as for all subsequent exercises.

```
apt-get update
```

(c) Tool installation

Enter the following command to install *cURL*. Select "yes" when prompted if you want to use additional disk space.

```
apt-get install curl
```

Next, install the Geth application. The Geth application is a distribution of Ethereum written in GO; this is the standard distribution and will serve our illustrative purposes well.

Use the *curl* command to download *Geth and tools* and save it to a file named *geth.tar.gz.*

```
curl -o geth.tar.gz https://gethstore.blob.core.windows.net/builds/geth-alltools-
linux-amd64-1.8.21-9dc5d1a9.tar.gz
```

Next, use the *tar* command to unpack the *geth-alltools.tar.gz* archive.

```
tar -C geth --strip-components 1 -xzf geth.tar.gz
```

Next, use the *cp* command to copy the *Geth* command line tools to the user programs folder on your simulated Ubuntu instance:

```
cp geth/* /usr/bin/
```

Next, use the *rm* command to delete the downloaded files. Note that this step is optional; you can also keep the archive on your computer.

```
rm -r geth geth.tar.gz
```

(d) Account creation

Next, you will use the *Official implementation of the Ethereum protocol, Geth*, to start a local Ethereum-based network. Initially, you will mine this network alone. For this, first create a new Ethereum account. You will use this account in this exercise to receive mining rewards and fees. For our illustrative purposes, this account will be unlocked by default so you can use it both to send and receive Ether.

To create a new Ethereum account on your local instance, use the following command. (The node_pow folder contains both the databases and keystore.)

```
geth account new --datadir node_pow
```

Next, you will be prompted to specify a passphrase. For now, you can press the enter key twice to skip this step, as we will not be using a password.

```
Your new account is locked with a password. Please give a password.

Do not forget this password.
Passphrase:
Repeat passphrase:
```

Now you will see your newly created Ethereum address displayed in the command line; it should look something like this:

```
Address: {e9c51fb5f23321142ee20e991413b956e1c5fbc6}
```

An Ethereum address is the public identifier for an account, and it is used to receive and spend Ether; the address is derived by taking the rightmost 160 bits (i.e., 20 byte) of the Keccak-256 hash of the account's public key (i.e., the public part of the Elliptic Curve Digital Signature Algorithm (ECDSA) key). Usually, the address is shown, as above, in hexadecimal format (i.e. base-16 notation). Each hexadecimal character represents 4 bits; thus, the total length of the address is 40 hexadecimal characters. A common convention to denote a hexadecimal string is to prefix it with "0x":

```
Address: {0xe9c51fb5f23321142ee20e991413b956e1c5fbc6}
```

You will notice that the above address is only 40 characters long because it is missing the 0x prefix. Thus, the address is really:

```
Address: {0xe9c51fb5f23321142ee20e991413b956e1c5fbc6}
```

(e) **Set up genesis**

Next you will configure and launch a private Ethereum network using the *puppeth* command. This step will include creating the first block of our own blockchain (hence, the name "genesis"). The genesis block forms the foundation of any blockchain system and is the prototype of all other blocks in the blockchain.

The *puppeth* command is used to assemble and maintain private networks:

```
puppeth
```

Next, you will be prompted to specify an Ethereum network name, type *node_pow*.

```
Please specify a network name to administer (no spaces or hyphens, please)
> node_pow
```

Next, you will be prompted to select an action; choose 2 to configure a new genesis.

```
What would you like to do? (default = stats)
 1. Show network stats
 2. Configure new genesis
 3. Track new remote server
 4. Deploy network components
> 2
```

Next, you will be prompted to specify what you want to do; choose 1 to create a new genesis block from scratch.

```
What would you like to do? (default = create)
 1. Create new genesis block from scratch
 2. Import already existing genesis
> 1
```

Next, you will be prompted to select a consensus algorithm; choose 1 to use proof-of-work (PoW):

```
Which consensus engine to use? (default = clique)
 1. Ethash - proof-of-work
 2. Clique - proof-of-authority
> 1
```

Next, you will be prompted to specify pre-funded accounts. Copy and paste the first address that you set up in step (d) so it gets pre-funded.

```
Which accounts should be pre-funded? (advisable at least one)
> 0xe9c51fb5f23321142ee20e991413b956e1c5fbc6
> 0x
```

You will now be asked if you want to pre-fund your initial address with 1 wei; type yes and press enter to pre-fund the address.

```
Should the precompile-addresses (0x1 .. 0xff) be pre-funded with 1 wei? (advisable yes)
> yes
```

Next, you will be prompted to specify a network identifier; type *101* and press enter:

```
Specify your chain/network ID if you want an explicit one (default = random)
> 101
```

Next, you will be prompted to select an action; choose 2 to manage the existing genesis.

```
What would you like to do? (default = stats)
 1. Show network stats
 2. Manage existing genesis
 3. Track new remote server
 4. Deploy network components
> 2
```

Next, you will be prompted to select an action; choose 2 to export the genesis.

```
 1. Modify existing fork rules
 2. Export genesis configuration
 3. Remove genesis configuration
> 2
```

You will now be prompted to select a folder in which to save the genesis specs; press enter to select the default (current) folder.

```
Which folder to save the genesis specs into? (default = current)
 Will create node_pow.json, node_pow-aleth.json, node_pow-harmony.json,
 node_pow-parity.json
```

Next, you will be prompted to select an action, press the key combination *Control + C* to exit *Geth*; after that, you should again see the root@… command prompt.

```
What would you like to do? (default = stats)
 1. Show network stats
 2. Manage existing genesis
 3. Track new remote server
 4. Deploy network components
> ^C
```

(f) **Create network**

Use *geth* to start a new network using the configured genesis.

```
geth init node_pow.json --datadir node_pow
```

(g) **Start network**

Next, use the *geth* command with the following parameters to start mining the first block of your very own blockchain:

```
geth --datadir node_pow --mine --miner.threads 1
```

When you start the network for the first time, you will have to create a DAG file. (We will not go into the technical specifics of DAG files at this point.) There are two main objectives for using a DAG file: to ensure ASIC-resistance (i.e., prevent individuals from building special-purpose mining hardware) and to allow for a less computationally intensive way for clients to verify mined blocks in the network. Depending on your hardware, generating the DAG file may take up to 30 minutes.

As the DAG file is being created, you should see something like this on your output screen:

```
INFO [09-14|16:42:21.554] Generating DAG in progress    epoch=0 percentage=2 elapsed=6.846s
INFO [09-14|16:42:23.921] Generating DAG in progress    epoch=0 percentage=3 elapsed=9.213s
INFO [09-14|16:42:26.248] Generating DAG in progress    epoch=0 percentage=4 elapsed=11.540s
INFO [09-14|16:42:28.468] Generating DAG in progress    epoch=0 percentage=5 elapsed=13.760s
INFO [09-14|16:42:30.768] Generating DAG in progress    epoch=0 percentage=6 elapsed=16.060s
```

After the creation of the DAG file is complete, your client node will automatically start the mining work. You will see the following output periodically for each block. You are now mining your very own blockchain!

```
INFO [09-14|16:56:03.375] Successfully sealed new block      number=49 sealhash=d0e…51a hash=ede…b9b elapsed=9.347s
INFO [09-14|16:56:03.375] 🔗 block reached canonical chain   number=42 hash=b02…413
INFO [09-14|16:56:03.375] 🔨 mined potential block           number=49 hash=ede…b9b
INFO [09-14|16:56:03.375] Commit new mining work            number=50 sealhash=18e…981 uncles=0 txs=0 gas=0 fees=0 elapsed=261.3µs
```

After mining a few blocks, you can exit the Geth console using the key combination *Control + C*.

Now, you should re-enter the Geth console—this time in the interactive mode so you can type commands to interact with the blockchain. For this, use the following command:

```
geth --verbosity 2 console --datadir node_pow --mine --miner.threads 1 --nousb
```

As a last step, we will stop the miner again before moving on to the next set of exercises in Chap. 2. You can stop the miner again with the following command:

```
> miner.stop();
```

You can use the following command at any point to determine whether your blockchain is actually being mined:

```
> eth.mining
false
```

In the exercises in Chap. 2, we will create more accounts, execute transactions, and analyze the metadata for both transactions and the individual blocks in more detail.

The starting point for each exercise in any chapter will be the state that we reached in the previous chapter. For example, the starting point for the Chap. 2 exercises is an individual Ethereum node that mines blocks with a PoW configuration (Sect. 1.7).

References

1. Held G (2003) The ABCs of TCP/IP. Auerbach, Boca Raton
2. Choudhry M (2012) The principles of banking. Wiley, Singapore
3. Martin F (2015) Money: the unauthorized biography from coinage to cryptocurrencies. Vintage Books, New York
4. Graeber D (2014) Debt: the first 5,000 years. Melville House, New York
5. Lewis A (2018) The basics of bitcoins and blockchains: an introduction to cryptocurrencies and the technology that powers them. Mango Media Inc, London
6. Popper N (2016) Digital gold: bitcoin and the inside story of the misfits and millionaires trying to reinvent money. HarperCollins, New York
7. Narayanan A, Bonneau J, Felten E et al (2016) Bitcoin and cryptocurrency technologies: a comprehensive introduction. Princeton University Press, Princeton
8. Menezes A, Van Oorschot P, Vanstone S (2001) Handbook of applied cryptography (Discrete mathematics and its applications). CRC Press, Middletown
9. Paar C, Pelzl J (2011) Understanding cryptography: a textbook for students and practitioners. Springer, Heidelberg
10. Nakamoto S (2018) Bitcoin: a peer-to-peer electronic cash system
11. Merkle R (1979) Secrecy, authentication, and public key systems. http://www.merkle.com/papers/Thesis1979.pdf

Cryptocurrencies

2.1 Introduction

A cryptocurrency is a currency in the digital realm that is designed to work as a medium of exchange. Entries of units—called tokens or crypto tokens—in a decentralized consensus-database (blockchain) make up the fabric of the cryptocurrency. As the name suggests, the construct underlying cryptocurrencies relies heavily on cryptography to ensure that transactions are verified and secure, and to control the supply of new units.

During the 1990s tech boom, pioneering entrepreneurs led the way with early attempts to launch crypto-based digital currencies. DigiCash, a company by David Chaum founded in 1989, put in the most substantial effort to that end [1]. Chaum's enterprise was unique in its quest to make transactions anonymous and, as such, it was a harbinger of what was to come [2]. In the end, Chaum proved to be ahead of his time and DigiCash, like most early efforts, did not survive.

One aspect that all these early efforts had in common was their reliance on a trusted intermediary or third party to verify and facilitate the trades, much like traditional banks have done for centuries. The next wave of digital currencies, spearheaded by Bitcoin, would do away with third-party intermediaries by using blockchain technology, thereby revolutionizing the concept of how a currency might function.

The earliest formalized idea for a decentralized digital currency based on cryptography dates to the end of the last century. In 1998, computer scientist Nick Szabo published a proposal [3] for an entirely digital currency named "bit gold." The currency contained no code at the time; it was just an idea. While Szabo never realized his concept, his idea paved the way for the cryptocurrency era, and when Bitcoin was launched in 2009, speculation was that Szabo might be behind the pseudonym Satoshi Nakamoto, the anonymous inventor of the Bitcoin protocol.

When decentralized cryptocurrencies eventually emerged, they did so as the byproduct of Bitcoin, which was announced as a "peer-to-peer electronic cash system." In retrospect, the single most impactful feature of this invention was its

© Springer Nature Switzerland AG 2020
D. Hellwig et al., *Build Your Own Blockchain*, Management for Professionals,
https://doi.org/10.1007/978-3-030-40142-9_2

decentralization, as it required neither central nodes nor a controlling authority. This approach resembles the P2P networks for file-sharing (e.g., Napster, BitTorrent), which revolutionized the entertainment industry in the early 2000s. (See Chap. 3.)

This chapter introduces the operability rules and conditions that are required to operate a cryptocurrency and considers how these mechanisms address the critical challenges that digital currencies face (as outlined in Chap. 1). We then delve into the cryptocurrency-mining process, and we review tokens and coins and what sets them apart. We end by outlining the practical aspects of owning cryptocurrencies, such as wallet technology and crypto ATMs.

2.1.1 Overview

Cryptocurrencies consist of a limited set of entries in a database, the digital equivalent of an accounting ledger. Cryptography-based principles control the creation of new entries (i.e., the origination of new currency units) and verify the transactions between users.

Since these entries are based on blockchain technology, they are unalterable once made; changes to the database can occur only by adding new ledger entries. For example, if someone transfers ten units of a cryptocurrency but meant to transfer eight, she cannot reverse the original transaction but must execute another transaction to have two units sent back if the other account owner agrees, thereby adding a new ledger entry. Contrast this process with those of traditional currencies and accounts, where an erroneous transfer can be corrected after the fact by canceling and re-executing it. Therefore, the blockchain network protocol creates a system in which certain conditions must be met before database changes can occur (e.g., account transfers, token origination).

Traditional accounts that are maintained by financial institutions are little more than ledger entries in a centralized database. As in the crypto world, financial institutions update bank account entries only under certain conditions. For example, a person can wire money to another account only if he has the money. In the case of traditional banks, these rules are captured in software code and are then enforced mechanically.

Some anticipate that a decentralized cryptocurrency implementation could one day replace real-world fiat currency transactions. To develop a good sense of what requirements and rules such an implementation must meet, let us first consider the key principles underlying the practical operations of decentralized cryptocurrencies.

2.1.2 Crypto Properties

The principles outlined below are the critical anchors required for the operation of decentralized cryptocurrencies:

- Irreversibility: Once confirmed, a transaction cannot be reversed, and the money is irretrievable. If a user sends funds to the wrong address, or a malicious actor steals them by transferring them using a stolen private key, then the rightful owner cannot retrieve his property: cryptocurrencies do not provide a safety net.
- Pseudonymity: With cryptocurrencies, there is no direct link between accounts or individual transactions to user identities in the real world. Network participants can receive tokens (e.g., bitcoins) using addresses. While it is technically possible to analyze the historical transactions of all users (i.e., to find groupings of accounts that transact with each other or to infer information about an account holder's location from transaction time analysis), without additional data (e.g., IP records from internet providers) it is not possible to connect cryptocurrency addresses to the identities of the corresponding users.
- Propagation: Transactions are broadcast almost instantly to all nodes in a network and are then confirmed as quickly as possible. For Bitcoin, the confirmation process (i.e., inclusion into the next block) usually takes about ten minutes. The global nature of a cryptocurrency network makes it location-agnostic: Whether a transaction originated from a next-door neighbor or someone on another continent is irrelevant to network operations.
- Security: Cryptocurrency funds are protected through asymmetric cryptography. Thus, any cryptocurrency can be controlled by anyone who holds the private key that corresponds to an address. Advanced cryptography methods make it impossible to break this scheme in finite time using technology that is available today. (See Chap. 8.)
- Permissionless: In a trustless cryptocurrency network, users do not have to obtain permission to participate, so anyone can join and exchange cryptocurrency tokens (e.g., bitcoins). Without an official gatekeeper, there is no formal way to prevent anyone from participating.

Next, we consider how simple transactions play out in a decentralized system by looking at the mechanisms that asymmetric keys enable for message validation and control.

2.1.3 Transactions

As outlined in Chap. 1, anyone in the network can see the balance of every account and verify the integrity of the ledger without relying on a third party. In a decentralized network like Bitcoin, every network node (i.e., every participating computer) performs the task of keeping records of transactions and balances. Blockchain technology helps to organize this collective process by functioning as a public ledger and keeping track of the records of every transaction that has ever taken place on the network.

The creation of a new Bitcoin account triggers the creation of two keys: A private key, which is held by the account owner, and a public key, which is shared with the entire blockchain network on request [4].

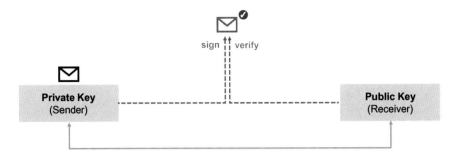

Fig. 2.1 Digital signatures

A transaction is a message that says, "Daniel gives X bitcoins to Max." Daniel signs this message using his private key, which is the primary mechanism of public-key cryptography. After Daniel signs the message (i.e., provides the transaction instruction), the message is broadcast to the network and is sent from one peer to another until every peer node has received it. This is basic P2P technology.

Each Bitcoin transaction contains the public key of the sender, the address of the recipient, and the number of bitcoins to move. In addition, the sender must use his private key to provide a cryptographic signature (as discussed in Chap. 8), which is how the sender authorizes a transaction (Fig. 2.1). Once validated, the network broadcasts the transaction with all its information to the other nodes in the network for validation. The sender considers the transaction confirmed once the majority of the other network nodes has reviewed and accepted it.

2.1.4 Double Spending

Perhaps the most critical issue faced by any digital currency is double-spending, that is, the fraudulent spending of the same unit of currency more than once [5]. In the real world, it is practically impossible to use the same dollar bill more than once, as after a bill has been handed over to a merchant, it is physically gone; it is not possible to use that same bill again unless the original owner retrieves it physically, whether lawfully or unlawfully.

In the digital realm, however, double-spending is possible. For example, one can send a digital music file to many recipients without altering the immediate value of each individual file; after the data is transferred, one cannot tell the data files apart. Unfortunately for the music owner, the song will lose value, as no one will pay for it anymore. This scenario presented a considerable challenge for the entertainment industry at the end of the last century, disrupting the music business and resulting in new economic models (e.g., iTunes, Spotify).

The most common approach to preventing double-spending was once tasking a third-party service to keep records of all balances and transactions. However, this approach runs counter to the nature of decentralized cryptocurrencies, as it

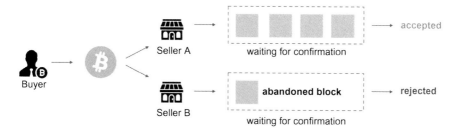

Fig. 2.2 Double-spending

necessitates a central authority that controls all funds and is privy to all personal information about the individuals who participate in a transaction. As a result, before the advent of Bitcoin, the double-spending problem had rendered the concept of decentralized digital money largely unfeasible.

So how do decentralized cryptocurrencies address the issue of double-spending (Fig. 2.2)? All participants in the network has a record of all transactions that have ever occurred in the system, so they can each derive the cryptocurrency balance of any participating account. Briefly, since units of cryptocurrency are identifiable on the blockchain, when a user wants to spend a unit, the network can look up whether the unit has already been transferred to someone else and withhold authorization for the transaction. Thus, the problem of double-spending is effectively resolved.

2.2 Miners

2.2.1 Process Overview

Next, we will consider the mechanisms that control and enable changes in the blockchain-based databases (or ledgers). All cryptocurrencies like Bitcoin are enabled by a network of peers who run and operate the network infrastructure with their computers.

In the Bitcoin ecosystem, the nodes ("miners") confirm transactions by using their computing power to solve calculations. The mining process involves grouping transactions into blocks, validating them, and then spreading them across the network for validation by other nodes.

When other nodes confirm the validity of a block, they add its transactions to their local database, also known as a ledger. Once more than half of the network confirms a set (block) of transactions, it becomes permanent and irreversible. The miner who first solved the math puzzle receives a reward and applicable fees for the transactions that are included in the block.

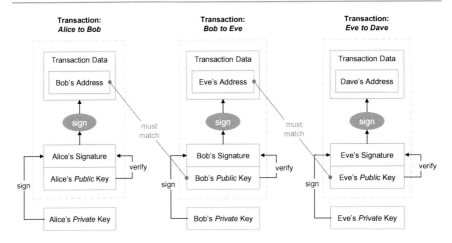

Fig. 2.3 Diagram of a Bitcoin transfer protocol

The validity of a cryptocurrency network and, thus, the validity of its balances and transactions, relies on the consensus of the nodes that make up a specific blockchain system. The integrity of the system breaks down if the network nodes do not reach consensus with regard to the balance of every account, but safeguards are programmed into the client software run by the nodes to avoid such a break.

The mechanisms of transaction confirmations and the mining of cryptocurrencies are closely related (Fig. 2.3). The continuous mining process that is run by all participating nodes in the network executes the bitcoin transactions. The next two sections consider each process separately.

2.2.2 Transaction Confirmation

Following the P2P-based process we just reviewed, a transaction message is available to the entire network almost immediately. However, transactions are confirmed only shortly thereafter (about 10 minutes in the case of Bitcoin). What accounts for this gap?

The key is that miners need both receive the transaction information and to confirm it. Miners select a series of unconfirmed transactions (usually about 10,000 in the case of Bitcoin), confirm that they are formally valid (e.g., that the sender has enough bitcoins to cover the transaction), group them as one block, and only then broadcast them back to the entire network, after which every node must add the block to its local database. Only at that point has the transaction become part of the blockchain. The miners are rewarded for performing this task, receiving, in the case of Bitcoin, both a mining reward (i.e., a pre-set number of new coins) and the transaction fees for the transaction they confirmed.

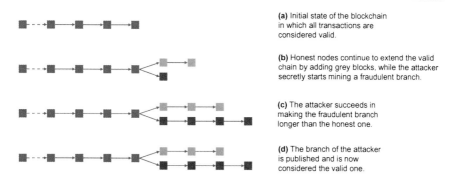

(a) Initial state of the blockchain in which all transactions are considered valid.

(b) Honest nodes continue to extend the valid chain by adding grey blocks, while the attacker secretly starts mining a fraudulent branch.

(c) The attacker succeeds in making the fraudulent branch longer than the honest one.

(d) The branch of the attacker is published and is now considered the valid one.

Fig. 2.4   Conceptual visualization of a 51% attack

Confirmation is a critical step. If a transaction is unconfirmed, it is considered to be pending and can, in theory, be forged via double-spending, although most nodes will reject an attempt to issue another transaction that spends the same funds again. Once the network confirms a transaction, it becomes permanent and irreversible, as it has become part of a block that contains a permanent record of past transactions (i.e., a block of the blockchain). Changing any data element of this transaction after this point would require the recalculation of *all* transactions that come afterward as well, a task that is practically infeasible.

In the unlikely event of a rogue actor's succeeding in taking over more than half of the nodes in a network, the network may become corrupted in what is known as a 51% attack. (See Fig. 2.4.)

2.2.3   Mining Process

Since the activity of the miners is the single most crucial element in the Bitcoin ecosystem and other cryptocurrency ecosystems, let us delve a little deeper into the responsibilities of the miners and the nature of their tasks.

In principle, anyone who participates in a network can act as a miner. A decentralized network relies exclusively on its miners to enforce the rules of the network, as the mining task cannot be performed by external actors. A cryptocurrency network also requires a mechanism to prevent the establishment of a majority, as such a majority could abuse its power to alter the state of the network. For example, if a single party were to control the majority of nodes in a network, as in a 51% attack, it could change the state of the network (e.g., historical transactions), rendering the entire operation obsolete, as the integrity of the system would be compromised. In the past, large mining pools have voluntarily split up to prevent too much mining concentration in the network.

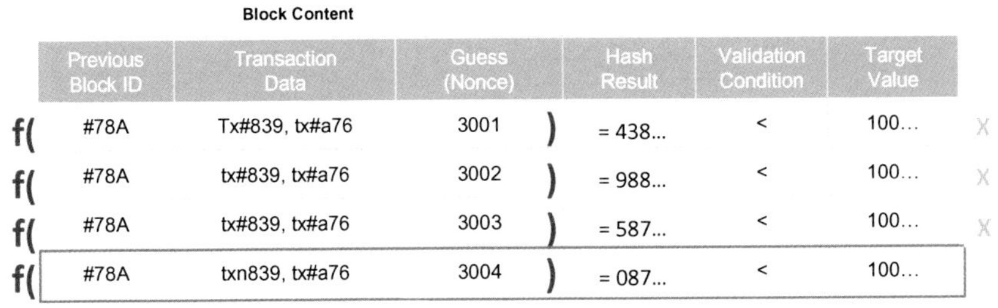

Block Content

	Previous Block ID	Transaction Data	Guess (Nonce)		Hash Result	Validation Condition	Target Value	
f(	#78A	Tx#839, tx#a76	3001	)	= 438...	<	100...	X
f(	#78A	tx#839, tx#a76	3002	)	= 988...	<	100...	X
f(	#78A	tx#839, tx#a76	3003	)	= 587...	<	100...	X
f(	#78A	txn839, tx#a76	3004	)	= 087...	<	100...	

Fig. 2.5 Hash validation of the Bitcoin mining process

For Bitcoin, miners invest computing capacity to perform the task of validating transactions. Once miners have selected 10,000 transactions and grouped them into a block, they must find the corresponding hash, the primary purpose of which is to link the new block of selected transactions with the previous block, a process called Proof-of-Work (PoW). Bitcoin uses the SHA256 hashing algorithm.

The details of the SHA 256 algorithm are beyond the scope of this introduction; suffice it to say that this algorithm forms the basis for the cryptographic puzzle that all miners must solve as part of the Bitcoin mining process (Fig. 2.5). New blocks can be added to the blockchain only once a miner has solved the puzzle by finding the correct hash for the collection of transactions that he or she selected. The miner who finds the right solution first is rewarded with the transaction fees of the block and via the so-called coinbase transaction [6], which gives the miner a certain number of bitcoins as a reward for her mining efforts. The difficulty of the cryptographic puzzle changes proportionately to the amount of computer power that all miners invest collectively, thus regulating the number of new cryptocurrency units that the network can create in a set amount of time. The coinbase transaction is the only way to originate new bitcoins.

2.2.4 The Nonce

In cryptography, a nonce (perhaps originating from "number used once") is a random number that is used only once for a particular purpose [7]. It is used in authentication protocols like TLS (HTTPS) handshakes to ensure the uniqueness and, thus, the non-repeatability of the procedure. As such, using a nonce twice may weaken the underlying network protocol.

In Bitcoin, miners use the nonce to produce a hash that is less than or equal to the target hash. The hash value of a block must meet precise specifications in the blockchain. For example, the hash in Bitcoin must start with a certain number of zeros, and the higher the number of the hash's leading zeros, the greater the difficulty of finding it.

Therefore, in addition to its other data, a block also contains a "nonce" field. To illustrate, let's assume the current difficulty (defined by the blockchain protocol) is 00, the randomly generated nonce is 2983373116, and the given data is The quick brown fox jumps over the lazy dog. These assumptions would result in the following SHA256 hash:

```
EF537F25C895BFA782526529A9B63D97AA631564D5D789C2B765448C8635FB6C
```

Since the hash will change unpredictably if either the nonce or the data changes, the more zeros that are required for the hash prefix (i.e., the difficulty), the more computationally intensive it is to find a nonce that results in such a hash value.

Verifying whether a chosen nonce and the given data result in an acceptable hash value is relatively easy, but finding a nonce that will result in an acceptable hash— that is, the mining process—is computationally expensive.

2.3   Coins and Tokens

2.3.1   Introduction

The term *cryptocurrency* usually covers both coins and tokens. However, most coins do not perform as currencies, as they are not necessarily a medium of exchange. For example, a coin may have no value whatsoever if it acts as a certificate for an object in the real world. In that sense, the term *cryptocurrency* is a misnomer when applied to coins, as a currency must represent a unit of account, a store of value, and a medium of exchange.

Bitcoin, Ethereum, and other digital coins fulfill these requirements, but most of the hundreds of crypto coins available today do not, so they should not be considered cryptocurrencies.

For the purposes of this book, we categorize cryptocurrencies as coins (i.e., a digital unit unique to its own blockchain), altcoins (an abbreviation for "alternative cryptocurrency coins"), and tokens. The specific setup of the underlying technical infrastructure provides the differentiation between altcoins and tokens. While tokens leverage existing blockchains, usually the Ethereum blockchain, altcoins operate in their separate infrastructure (i.e., blockchain).

As of today, most coins are tokens, as the process for originating them is simple; they just use the existing infrastructure of another cryptocurrency, such as Bitcoin or Ethereum. The next two sections explain the differences between them. Readers can launch a new token themselves as part of this chapter's practical exercises.

2.3.2 Altcoins

Most altcoins in circulation today are so-called forks (variants) of Bitcoin. The term *fork* describes an entirely separate instance of a crypto coin that relies on the Bitcoin protocol, with slight variations [8]. Such an approach is possible because the Bitcoin project follows the principles of open-source development. Indeed, anyone can freely download, modify, and use the underlying software to launch a cryptocurrency project. Thus, conceiving an entirely new coin that is based on a separate block-chain and constructed using a different set of features has become relatively easy.

Some altcoins do not rely on Bitcoin's open-source protocol. The best-known example is Ethereum, which runs a separate blockchain and protocol that has little to do with the original Bitcoin baseline. Ethereum is unique because it allows the inclusion of complex logic ("smart contracts"); Chap. 4 covers this topic in more detail.

The critical commonality of all altcoins is that they all have their independent blockchains, and any transaction that occurs uses that blockchain's native coins.

2.3.3 Tokens

Tokens, by definition, represent a specific asset or utility (e.g., loyalty points, commodities, ownership shares)—any assets that are fungible and tradable. Unlike altcoins, tokens usually leverage an already existing blockchain (e.g., Bitcoin, Ethereum).

Originating tokens is a much simpler process than originating altcoins is, as issuing a token does not require modifying the underlying protocol or launching a separate blockchain from scratch. Instead, an individual who wants to create a new token can follow a standard, template-based approach. This process takes only hours using an existing blockchain platform like Ethereum.

Tokens can be created by using smart contracts: computer programs that are self-executing and do not need third parties to operate (Fig. 2.6; see Chap. 4).

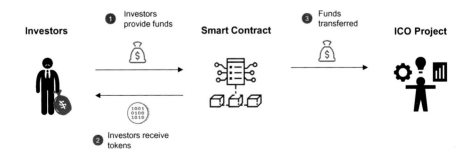

Fig. 2.6 Origination of tokens

The most prominent use case for tokens is the so-called Initial Coin Offering (ICO), a means of crowdfunding that is based on the controlled release of a new cryptocurrency or token, usually to fund the development of a new project [9]. The process resembles the initial public offerings (IPOs) that companies use to trade their stocks publicly, but ICOs initially were not subject to the same regulatory requirements and disclosures that IPOs are. As of today, regulatory rules vary by country: for example, in the United States, the SEC has issued a statement deeming all ICOs as security offerings like IPOs unless there is a sufficient degree of decentralization present before the sale (which was the case for Ethereum, while everyone else is paying securities violations fines today).

2.3.4 ERC-20 Standard

The most popular form of tokens on the Ethereum Blockchain is the Ethereum Request for Comments-20 (ERC-20) token. ERC-20 is an official Ethereum standard that Fabian Vogelsteller and Vitalik Buterin published at the end of 2015, and it is the officially accepted protocol for the commands any token must implement to be able to fulfill the ERC-20 token standard [10].

The driving motivation for the ERC-20 standard is to provide an interface that allows any token on Ethereum to be re-used by other applications, from wallets to decentralized exchanges. This standard provides basic functionality for token transfers and approvals. With this approval, any on-chain third party can use and spend the token.

To understand all the implications of ERC-20, one must first understand the Ethereum blockchain. (See Chap. 4.) We can summarize the Ethereum system as one that engenders programmable money; since the ERC-20 tokens rely on the Ethereum platform principles, they also become programmable tokens. The outcome is that the designer can customize a token in infinite but predictable ways.

The standard specifies an application programming interface (API) that allows developers to issue their standardized tokens, thus formalizing the methods of these smart contract-based tokens. This approach also allows third-party vendors to read the information and perform the transactions accurately, since the same set of program functions is used for each ERC-20 token. A third-party app can be programmed generically for each ERC-20 token without knowing the specific token.

The ERC-20 token standard also contains the necessary modalities that a token should implement for it to start trading after launch, namely, transferring tokens, inquiring about balances for specified addresses, and determining the total token supply. Table 2.1 provides an overview of the standard methods that ERC-20 token must implement to be valid [11].

Similarly, there are events that every ERC-20 token must implement [12]. Events can be "listened to" (i.e., tracked and processed by another computer), and actors can receive a constant stream of information about the token's digital state so

Table 2.1 Overview of standard ERC-20 methods

Method	Description
Name	Returns the name of the token (e.g., "MyToken")
Symbol	Returns the symbol of the token (e.g., "HIX")
Decimals	Returns the number of decimals the token uses (e.g., 8)
TotalSupply	Returns the total token supply (the total number of tokens)
BalanceOf	Returns the number of tokens owned by an account (i.e., address)
Transfer	Transfers a specified number of tokens to an account
TransferFrom	Transfers a specified number of tokens from one account to another
Approve	Approves pre-approval of transfers from one account to another
Allowance	Returns the remaining pre-approved amount to transfer

Table 2.2 Overview of standard ERC-20 events

Event	Description
Transfer	Triggered when tokens are transferred, including zero-value transfers
Approval	Triggered upon any successful call to approve

any participant who is listening to the event will be notified of a change in the state of the token. Table 2.2 summarizes the transfer and approval events.

ERC-20 is a technical standard that specifies a programmatic interface that a new token on the platform needs to support. Before the ERC-20 standard was defined, tokens that had been developed based on the Ethereum blockchain had to implement their bespoke functionalities, so different tokens behaved differently on the network. For example, their transfer functions were implemented differently, required different attributes, and followed different rules and logic. As a result, tokens had to draw up individual contracts to ensure interoperability, a complexity that increased with the number of tokens on the network. Only the introduction of the ERC-20 standard ensured broad interoperability among the various tokens.

The ERC-20 token standard ensures that new tokens will not interfere with but can still interoperate with any existing tokens on a network and that new tokens are automatically compatible. For example, by following the ERC-20 token standard, the tokens issued from a new ICO can be included/traded on any exchange without having to create bilateral agreements between the token issuer and the exchange operator.

2.4 Market Makers/Exchanges

2.4.1 Introduction

The last two sections of this chapter outline the practical aspects of owning cryptocurrencies, such as wallet technology and crypto ATMs.

Fig. 2.7 Bitcoin and Ethereum ATMs in Hong Kong

Individuals can acquire bitcoins in several ways. Countries like Switzerland and Canada allow for the placement of cryptocurrency ATMs. Today, there are approximately 2000 Bitcoin ATMs spread over more than fifty countries (Fig. 2.7). People can also buy bitcoins using brokers, online exchanges, decentralized exchanges, trading platforms, and offline trading. This section discusses these possibilities in detail.

The buying options are not as diverse for other, less popular cryptocurrencies. The range of purchasing methods depends on the currencies used, their popularity, and the physical location of the purchaser.

2.4.2   Brokers

Face-to-face trading is not a popular way of receiving coins, so brokers are web-based exchanges that allow customers to buy and sell cryptocurrencies at a fixed price set by the broker (usually the market price plus a small premium). In this type of set-up, the exchange is between the buyer and the broker or the seller and the broker, not directly between the buyer and the seller. The broker approach is the simplest solution for new users, but buyers usually pay somewhat higher prices than they would on other types of exchange for the ease of use and the work that the broker puts in. The company Coinbase is a prominent example of this type of exchange.

2.4.3 Traditional Exchanges

Traditional exchanges are like conventional stock exchanges: they match buyers and sellers based on the current market price of a given currency. The exchange platform performs the function of the intermediary who runs the book. The traditional trading platform usually charges a transaction fee.

Some exchanges facilitate only cryptocurrency transactions, while others also provide means for trading fiat currencies (e.g., USD) for cryptocurrencies (e.g., BTC). Prominent examples of traditional exchanges are Coinbase's GDAX and the Kraken platform.

2.4.4 Decentralized Exchanges

A decentralized exchange (DEX) is a swap exchange that has no single point of potential failure. While smart contracts govern exchange operations without using centralized third-party software, and traditional centralized exchanges require specific user information (e.g., verification of identity via passport validation) but often allow fiat trading, DEX exchanges do not enable fiat trading but require little to no personal information.

DEX exchanges do not perform a trustee function, there is no registration or authentication process, and user information is not stored. Instead, it is a log that each user runs on his computer individually.

For a DEX to be decentralized, it must meet two conditions: no third-party intermediary, as money must stay with the trading parties, and no central servers, as a centralized server would be a single point of failure.

Few DEX exchanges exist today, but participants can remain anonymous using the Onion Router network (TOR); we will discuss anonymity in more detail in Chap. 5. With TOR, users operate their nodes, and all communication is encrypted end-to-end [12]. In other words, the exchanging parties are the only ones who have information about each other. For physical and digital goods, as well as services, there is OpenBazaar; for cryptocurrencies, there are BISQ and BitShares. Both are desktop applications that automatically set up a TOR node and connect to the other network participants.

2.4.5 Trading Platforms

A cryptocurrency trading platform is roughly comparable to a cryptocurrency stock exchange. These platforms offer direct peer-to-peer trading between buyers and sellers, who can sell crypto funds they own, exchange them for other means of payment, or even buy a new cryptocurrency. Trading platforms do not rely on a pre-set market price; sellers set their rates, and buyers connect with them using the platform or execute over-the-counter (OTC) transactions.

As in a traditional marketplace, users can obtain an overview of what the current cryptocurrency offering is (i.e., its market price) and what currencies they can use to purchase them. A cryptocurrency trading platform is the linchpin of transactions, as it allows users to make money from crypto funds by investing them.

2.4.6   Offline Exchanges

Bitcoins can also be purchased on the internet. For instance, the Bitcoin community has frequent meetings where the cryptocurrency can be purchased for cash. An offline exchange can be compared to a flea market, where buyers and sellers meet in person to transact between currencies—a type of trade that is unregulated.

2.5   Wallets

2.5.1   Introduction

Since bitcoins cannot be stored, crypto wallets offer a way to capture private keys that provide access to the public Bitcoin address and make transactions possible. There are various types of Bitcoin wallets, each of which has its own requirements and varies in terms of data security, ease of use, and technical simplicity.

2.5.2   Hardware Wallets

A hardware wallet is a unique form of bitcoin wallet that stores the private keys on secure hardware. It is the surest way to secure any number of bitcoins, as there have been no reported cases of malicious actors stealing money from a hardware wallet (yet). Hardware wallets are also immune to computer viruses, and it is impossible to read the stored keys in unencrypted form from the device. Hardware wallet devices generally use open-source software (e.g., TREZOR) for their operations, providing additional confidence, as the public can verify the software's integrity.

Each private key is derived from a random number generated using a pseudo-random number generator (PRNG) that was initialized ("seeded") with a seed, which is simply the initial state of the PRNG—that is, the seed is akin to the "initial" or "zeroth" random number in a PRNG generated sequence—and is isolated in the hardware wallet. The seed of the private keys is different from what is sometimes called the "recovery seed," which is used to recover a hardware wallet (i.e., to reset an existing hardware wallet or initialize a new hardware wallet) such that it has the same initial state and, thus, generates the same private key that was generated before on the lost or broken device.

The recovery seed is usually represented as a sequence of 12 (for 128 bits) or 24 (for 256 bits) words from a predefined dictionary of 2,048 words. (2,048 words is

11 bits, as $2^{\wedge}11 = 2{,}048$. $\text{Log}2(2048) = 11$, so $12 * 11 = 132$ bits, which is 128 bits seed + 4 bits checksum—or $24 * 11 = 264$ bits, which is 256 bit seed + 8 bits checksum.) The generation of the recovery mnemonic, also known as a recovery seed/phrase, is standardized for each blockchain. An example of such a mnemonic is BIP39 for Bitcoin wallets.

The security now is that a collection of private keys is stored on the hardware only: they are "software-isolated," and no private key ever leaves the hardware wallet. Transactions are verified and signed on the device; to withdraw from an exchange, a request is sent to transfer the asset to a public address provided by your hardware wallet.

Some hardware wallets have screens, adding another layer of security, as they can be used to view and verify essential wallet details. For example, a display may be used to query a password to confirm the amount and address of the payment.

Although not as conveniently accessible, especially compared to software or exchange wallets, hardware devices eliminate the need for trust between a crypto owner and the exchange: rather than trusting someone else (i.e., the exchange) to safeguard the currency units, an owner holds the tokens (i.e., the private keys) directly and does not have to worry about her tokens being stolen by third-party attackers that penetrate the exchange's infrastructure. Even if attackers manage to hack into a computer, they will not be able to transfer the user's coins without the correct passphrase.

2.5.3 Software Wallets

Another type of crypto wallet used for storing digital currency is a software wallet, which is a simple app that users download and run on their PCs.

Software wallets store the private keys on the user's local hard disc and are safer than online wallets because they do not trust third parties and are more difficult to steal. However, because of their connection to the internet, they are fundamentally unsafe, so desktop wallets are an excellent solution for those who send small amounts of bitcoins from their PCs.

Desktop wallets can cover various needs. Some specialize in security, others in anonymity. The main issue with these wallets is that they are susceptible to any hacker, malware, or virus that may gain access to an individual's computer. Any recovery phrase or passcode that may be visible on a screen could be seen and recorded by a hacker or stolen using spyware.

2.5.4 Exchange Wallets

Online wallets provide access to cryptocurrencies from any device connected to the internet. They offer convenience in that a user does not have to install software and can access the wallet via any internet browser. Online wallets store private keys on a server that is owned and operated by the companies that own the online wallet software.

Like mobile wallets, e-wallets give users access from any Internet-enabled device. However, if the company has not implemented the software correctly, the organization that operates the website can access users' private keys and have complete control over their money.

Exchange wallets are the least safe method for storing currencies, as the exchange stores the currency for the user, who can access the funds only via the online platform. Contrary to the usual rule for cryptocurrencies, exchange wallets introduce a single point of failure by acting as a third-party middleman, so if the exchange is compromised, a user can irreversibly lose her crypto assets.

The biggest failure of a crypto exchange was the unwinding of Mt. Gox. A Tokyo-based company founded in July 2010, Mt. Gox was handling more than 70 percent of all Bitcoin transactions by early 2014, but in February 2014, following the theft of approximately 850,000 bitcoins that belonged to customers and the company, Mt. Gox suspended trading, closed its website, and filed for bankruptcy protection [13].

While exchanges and other intermediaries in the cryptocurrency space have failed on multiple occasions over the past decade, there has been no successful attack on the core Bitcoin technology framework since its inception in 2009.

2.6 Exercise

2.6.1 Introduction

This chapter's exercise focuses on the creation of new accounts on the Ethereum blockchain. We will then move funds between the accounts, and demonstrate different scenarios and their impact (e.g., sending funds with and without a transaction fee). Throughout the exercises, we will periodically analyze the chart of accounts on our blockchain (i.e., review how much money is associated with each address). Following the money in this fashion will allow the reader to obtain a hands-on understanding of how funds move within the blockchain realm. Finally, we will look at one of the blocks containing one of the exercise transactions to provide a concrete example of exactly what data is captured as part of the transaction.

2.6.2 Standard Transfer

(a) **Reconnecting your Docker instance**

If you completed the exercise in Chap. 1, you can continue from there. If you exited the docker instance after completing the exercise in Chap. 1, you will need to start and reconnect to the console using the start and attach commands below. If your docker instance is still running, you can skip this step and continue with step (b).

Otherwise, please complete (or redo) all the steps from Chap. 1. For all the steps in this chapter, we assume that we are set up and ready to go with a PoW-based setup.

If you completed the exercise in Chap. 1, the docker instance will still be there. You can always see all your docker instances by typing the following command in the system console (i.e., your Windows command line or macOS terminal). Using the following command will show you all existing docker instances:

```
docker ps -a

CONTAINER ID    IMAGE     COMMAND        CREATED          STATUS          PORTS        NAMES
db253cb81bf7    ubuntu    "/bin/bash"    44 seconds ago   Exited (127)                 node_pow
```

If your console is not running, re-start the instance using the following command. Note that the container ID will be different:

```
docker start db253cb81bf7
root@db253cb81bf7:/#
```

Once your node is up and running (or if your node status is *running*), you can re-connect to the console using the following command. (Again, your container ID will be different):

```
docker attach db253cb81bf7
db253cb81bf7
```

At this point, you should be back at the @root screen; your prompt should look like this:

```
root@015e2e8bef67:/#
```

(b) **Interacting with the blockchain**

As a first step, we will re-launch the geth console. The geth console works just like the Ubuntu console. For the next few chapters, we will use it to interact with the blockchain that we are running locally on our computer.

The command below launches the Geth console in an interactive mode and with limited verbosity, meaning we will not see all of the mining output. Make sure that you are in the test1 folder before executing this command (by using the change directory (*cd*) command that we introduced in Chap. 1):

```
root@015e2e8bef67:~/test1#geth --verbosity 2 console --datadir node_pow --mine --miner.threads 1 --nousb
```

(c)   **Accounts and balances**

At any point, you can look at what accounts are on your blockchain; this is helpful for this exercise because you can track them individually. Once a transaction involving one or more of your accounts occurs, these changes will be captured on the actual blockchain as well.

To see what accounts exist already, you can use the personal.listAccounts command from within the Geth console:

```
> personal.listAccounts
[
    "0xe9c51fb5f23321142ee20e991413b956e1c5fbc6"
]
```

As above, you should be seeing two accounts. These are the two accounts that you created and pre-funded as part of the Chap. 1 exercises. As a next step, let us validate the value contained in each of these two accounts. For this, you will use the web3.eth.getBalance command.

Next, using the getBalance command, you can check the account balance of your individual accounts; it will be displayed in wei, the smallest unit in the Ether realm:

```
> web3.eth.getBalance("0xe9c51fb5f23321142ee20e991413b956e1c5fbc6")
396000000000000000000
```

For simplicity, you can write the same prompt by referencing one of your accounts via a parameter and the personal.listAccounts function; this will yield the same result:

```
> web3.eth.getBalance(personal.listAccounts[0])
396000000000000000000
```

(d)   **Your first transaction**

Before we create our first transaction, we will create an additional account. This account will not be pre-funded, making it easier for us to validate whether a transaction took place. From the Geth console, use the following command to create a new account:

```
> personal.newAccount()
Passphrase:
Repeat passphrase:
"0xa53f495b27a40b73e0919b89aa8e15d5c220199b"
```

At any point, you can look again at what accounts exist; there should now be three accounts: the two accounts that you created in Chap. 1 and the new (empty) account that you just created:

```
> personal.listAccounts
[
    "0xe9c51fb5f23321142ee20e991413b956e1c5fbc6",
    "0x24d016d3968facdf2c7f2c074522f1b92ce9ec30",
    "0xa53f495b27a40b73e0919b89aa8e15d5c220199b"
]
```

Next, using the getBalance command, you can verify that the latest account does not contain any ether:

```
> web3.eth.getBalance("0xa53f495b27a40b73e0919b89aa8e15d5c220199b")
0
```

For simplicity, you can write the same prompt by referencing one of your accounts via a parameter and the personal.listAccounts function; this will yield the same result:

```
> web3.eth.getBalance(personal.listAccounts[2])
0
```

Note also that you can use the "from wei" function to convert this number into Ether:

```
> web3.fromWei(web3.eth.getBalance(personal.listAccounts[0])),"Ether")
0
```

Next, we will execute our first transaction. For this, we need both a sender and a receiver address, as well as the private key of the sender. In the Geth command line, creating a new transaction works as follows:

```
web3.eth.sendTransaction
(
    {
        from:personal.listAccounts[0],
        to:personal.listAccounts[2],
        value:1000
    }
);
```

After trying this command, you will notice an error because you need to unlock the sender account first.

```
Error: authentication needed: password or unlock
    at web3.js:3143:20
    at web3.js:6347:15
    at web3.js:5081:36
    at <anonymous>:1:1
```

To do this, use the following prompt (and the password you set when you created this address):

```
> personal.unlockAccount(personal.listAccounts[0]);
Unlock account 0xe9c51fb5f23321142ee20e991413b956e1c5fbc6
Passphrase:
```

Now you should be able to conduct the transaction using web3.eth. sendTransaction:

```
web3.eth.sendTransaction

(

    {
        from:personal.listAccounts[0],

        to:personal.listAccounts[2],

        value:1000

    }

);
    "0x45b85025de231fd7641d475f0144bc130433cd843ea0190ac985b4734f889aa8"
```

The number displayed is the transaction hash; it can be used to identify any transaction conducted on the blockchain.

(e) **Transaction validation**

Next, let us re-validate the balance of both accounts to confirm that the transaction was carried out:

```
web3.eth.getBalance(personal.listAccounts[2]);
0
```

Hold on. What happened here? The balance in your sender accounts is still what it was before! This is because you were not mining the blockchain. For the transaction to *actually* occur, you need first to start the mining process.

At any point in time, you can use the following command to determine if your blockchain is actually being mined:

```
> eth.mining
false
```

Before we move to launch the mining process so we can finally send our transaction, let us look at the open transaction pool. Remember, these are the open transactions that have not yet been mined and so are not yet part of the blockchain.

```
> txpool.content
{
  pending: {
    0xE9c51fB5F23321142Ee20e991413b956e1C5fBC6: {
      0: {
        blockHash: "0x0000000000000000000000000000000000000000000000000000000000000000",
        blockNumber: null,
        from: "0xe9c51fb5f23321142ee20e991413b956e1c5fbc6",
        gas: "0x15f90",
        gasPrice: "0x3b9aca00",
        hash: "0x45b85025de231fd7641d475f0144bc130433cd843ea0190ac985b4734f889aa8",
        input: "0x",
        nonce: "0x0",
        r: "0xf289cc2cd78b4747b4cc28286551b6fdc0268d40781deb11d702828b372f0d8c",
        s: "0xa27f711d8db93dc26cef44b2640d6edc550f2949f3d9231df137f454315bd8",
        to: "0x24d016d3968facdf2c7f2c074522f1b92ce9ec30",
        transactionIndex: "0x0",
        v: "0xee",
        value: "0x3e8iner"
      }
    }
  },
  queued: {}
}
>
```

Next, we will start the mining process using the following command:

```
> miner.start();
```

You can stop the miner again with the following command:

```
> miner.stop();
```

At this point, we assume that our transaction was (1) mined, (2) included in a block, and (3) removed from the open transaction pool. Let's continue to validate these assumptions next.

```
> txpool.content
{
  pending: {},
  queued: {}
}
```

As you can see from the output, the open transaction pool is now empty; there are no pending transactions awaiting validation.

Next, let us confirm that the account balances were updated as expected. For this, we will enter the same command that we had tried before:

```
> web3.eth.getBalance(personal.listAccounts[0])
1000
```

Success! We can now see that the specified amount of 1,000 wei was transferred from our first personal account and sent to the third personal account we created.

In the exercises for Chap. 3, we will take a closer look at how the proof-of-authority (PoA) mechanism changes the process of mining blocks and confirming transactions.

References

1. Tapscott A, Tapscott D (2018) Blockchain revolution: how the technology behind bitcoin and other cryptocurrencies is changing the world. Penguin, New York City
2. Chaum D (1983) Blind signatures for untraceable payments. In: Advances in cryptology proceedings of crypto, vol 82, no 3, pp 199–203
3. Szabo N (2005) Bit gold. Retrieved 8 Jan 2017
4. Antonopoulos A (2017) Mastering bitcoin: unlocking digital cryptocurrencies. O'Reilly Media, Sebastopol
5. Narayanan A, Bonneau J, Felten E et al (2016) Bitcoin and cryptocurrency technologies: a comprehensive introduction. Princeton University Press, Princeton
6. Franco P (2015) Understanding bitcoin: cryptography, engineering and economics. Wiley, Chichester
7. Viega J, Messier M (2003) Secure programming cookbook for C and C++: recipes for cryptography, authentication, input validation & more. O'Reilly, New York
8. Diedrich H (2016) Ethereum: blockchains, digital assets, smart contracts, decentralized autonomous organizations. Wildfire Publishing, Brookvale
9. Werbach K (2018) The blockchain and the new architecture of digital trust. MIT Press, Cambridge
10. Mougayar W, Buterin V (2016) The business blockchain: promise, practice, and application of the next internet technology. Wiley, Hoboken
11. Wood G, Antonopoulos A (2019) Mastering Ethereum: building smart contracts and DApps. O'Reilly, Beijing
12. Bartlett J (2016) The dark net: inside the digital underworld. Melville House, Brooklyn
13. Popper N (2016) Digital gold: bitcoin and the inside story of the misfits and millionaires trying to reinvent money. HarperCollins, New York

Consensus Mechanisms

3

3.1 Introduction

One of blockchain's most prized features is the consistency—hence, the security—it provides to stored data. Consistency is achieved through consensus mechanisms, the most common of which is Bitcoin's Proof of Work (PoW) mechanism.

Consensus mechanisms incent desired behavior and dissuade participants from malicious actions by requiring participants to invest resources, be they computing capacity, storage capacity, a monetary stake, or the like.

This chapter first provides a formal definition of consensus algorithms and lists their objectives. Then it considers associated topics, such as the CAP theorem and Byzantine Fault. The chapter closes with an overview of the most common consensus mechanisms in use today, their strengths and weaknesses, and real-world examples that employ them.

3.1.1 Definition

In the blockchain world, consistency refers to an agreement among the various network nodes as to the state of the stored data, that is, all the changes that have taken place since the start of the particular blockchain and the sequence of these events. A consensus mechanism or protocol refers to the algorithm that reaches such an agreement on the status of a network. Consensus mechanisms are used in distributed systems, such as distributed ledgers, to ensure that all participants have an identical copy of the distributed database.

Distributed systems stand in stark contrast to centralized systems (e.g., banking databases), where one entity (e.g., the bank) has full control of the state of the data: such an entity could unilaterally alter a record (e.g., an account balance) without approval from anyone else. While such practices result in a loss of credibility and customers and are not in the bank's best interests, they are uncommon, but they are theoretically possible.

© Springer Nature Switzerland AG 2020

53

D. Hellwig et al., *Build Your Own Blockchain*, Management for Professionals,
https://doi.org/10.1007/978-3-030-40142-9_3

What follows is an overview of the objectives that a consensus mechanism must pursue to operate effectively in a distributed ledger network.

3.1.2 Objectives

At their core, consensus mechanisms aim to:

- **Achieve unified agreement**: The primary goal of any consensus mechanism is to solve the core problem that underlies distributed ledger systems, that is, to reach a unified agreement regarding the state of the network. By strictly following the protocol rules, nodes ensure that the network status is always current, that it is updated according to the latest agreement (consensus) reached by the majority of the network participants.
- **Prevent double-spending**: Chapter 2 introduced double-spending as one of the main problems faced by digital currencies. Consensus mechanisms address this problem by reviewing the history of all transactions in which a given coin has been involved and ensuring that only valid transaction messages are included in the public ledger.
- **Incent self-regulation**: The consensus mechanism supports the self-regulating aspects of a trustless system, which requires aligning the interests of all network participants. To that end, the mechanisms in place must incent desired behavior (e.g., through new token rewards) and punish rogue actors (e.g., by making dubious acts financially and computationally prohibitive). Thus, the consensus mechanism ensures that computing resources are better used in working for the system than against it. Network participants who are involved in consensus-building (i.e., the mining process) should be able to cover their expenses in the long term and earn rewards for the work that they do.
- **Ensure equality**: Blockchain is a peer-to-peer network with a low barrier to setting up new nodes and becoming a participant. Furthermore, anyone can review the underlying source code, as it is freely available, which allows the participants to directly validate the protocol's fairness. Thus, the consensus mechanism ensures that the blockchain is not discriminatory and that participants are treated equally.
- **Provide fault-tolerance**: In the computing space, fault tolerance describes a computer system whose design provides immediate and uninterrupted replacement in the event of a failure by resorting to backup components or other procedures. Consensus mechanisms ensure that blockchains remain reliable and consistent by being fault-tolerant.

3.1.3 Variations

Different blockchain implementations leverage different kinds of consensus algorithms. The Bitcoin blockchain, for instance, uses the Proof of Work (PoW) approach, whereas other blockchains deploy a variety of other algorithms depending on the blockchain's unique requirements. For example, the current implementation of the Bitcoin blockchain can, in theory, handle approximately 5–10 transactions per second [1], which suffices for value transfers but not for implementing a credit-card-like payment network, which requires the system to support much higher transaction numbers than Bitcoin does today. As a point of reference, the VISA network can handle approximately 10,000 transactions per second [2].

3.2 The CAP Theorem

3.2.1 The Trilemma

The CAP theorem, also known as Brewer's theorem [3], provides a theoretical basis for the unavoidable compromises that are inherent in distributed database systems, that is, their inability to obtain consistency, availability, and partition tolerance simultaneously (Fig. 3.1):

- **Consistency (C)**: Every retrieval from a node provides the most recent state of the system (i.e., the latest data). Unless the most recent information is available, the database will not return any response. Consistency requires that no two nodes in a network provide a different state at any point in time and that no node returns a non-current state.

Fig. 3.1 A Venn diagram of Brewer's CAP theorem

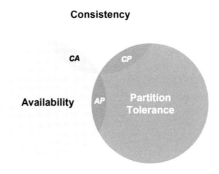

- **Availability (A)**: Every node in a system will always provide a (non-error) response. All nodes have constant read-and-write access: The system remains available, thereby enabling the user to make updates and retrieve data from the system at any time.
- **Partition tolerance (P)**: A partition describes the inability of two or more nodes of a network to communicate (i.e., messages delayed or dropped by the network between individual nodes). Partition tolerance refers to a network's ability to continue to operate despite the presence of partitions.

Illustration

Imagine a database that consists of a series of notebooks with recorded information. To achieve perfect consistency, you would use one notebook after another to write and read your notes. To read and write different information simultaneously, you would use multiple notebooks at once—perhaps one for each topic (availability)— and if the notebooks can be used in different rooms at the same time (partition tolerance), you would synchronize them from time to time to retain consistency.

According to the CAP theorem, a system can satisfy only two of these three properties at any one time; notably, that is not the case in Blockchain's most successful application to date, Bitcoin.

3.2.2   CAP Theorem and Blockchains

Blockchain networks like Bitcoin are distributed systems and so must contend with partition tolerance. Consequently, Bitcoin briefly sacrifices consistency in favor of availability and partition tolerance: Consistency (C) on the blockchain is not achieved simultaneously with partition tolerance (P) and availability (A) but is achieved over time. Eventual consistency describes a situation wherein consistency is achieved as a result of validation from multiple nodes in due course. For this purpose, Bitcoin introduced mining, which is a process that facilitates the achievement of consensus through the PoW algorithm (see Sect. 3.4.1), which facilitates the addition of more blocks.

Had Bitcoin instead chosen consistency over availability, a user would not be able to send or receive Bitcoins in the event of a connectivity problem or a failing node.

The primary function of a consensus algorithm is to provide eventual consistency for the data in the distributed blockchain database. The next sections describe and formalize the CAP theorem and provide solutions to the problems of decentralized networks—solutions that enable the operation of a reliable distributed ledger system for cryptocurrencies.

3.2.3 CAP Theorem in Practice

To illustrate the CAP theorem at work, we present a variety of scenarios in which selecting for two properties necessitates compromising on the third.

Scenario 1: Partition-tolerant and available, but not consistent
Consider the following scenario: Two states are stored in different nodes of a blockchain-based decentralized database, and four network nodes make up the network (Fig. 3.2). The account balance in each of these network nodes is USD 20.

Say I receive a wire transfer for an additional USD 10. Referring to Fig. 3.2, this wire transfer is first reflected in the node in the upper-left corner (depicted as state B). The node then shares this information with all other nodes in the network with which it can communicate. The new state of the node does not spread to all remaining nodes because of the partition between the left-hand side and the right-hand side. Thus, the latest balance update does not spread to the nodes on the right-hand side, and only the bottom-left node receives the message and reflects the most recent network state.

While not a single node in the network will return an error message, some might return non-current states.

Scenario 2: Partition-tolerant and consistent, but not available
Consider a starting configuration that is identical to that in the first scenario, except that the network is partitioned vertically such that only the two nodes on the left-hand side and the two nodes on the right-hand side can communicate (Fig. 3.3).

Given that we now require consistency—that is, for every node to return only the most recent state—availability must be sacrificed. Referring to Fig. 3.3, in this case, node 2 will return an error, as it cannot validate that it has the latest data that is consistent across the system because it cannot query all other nodes for their most recent state. Since it cannot receive messages from all nodes, it will assume that it is not up to date and will return an unavailability error as well.

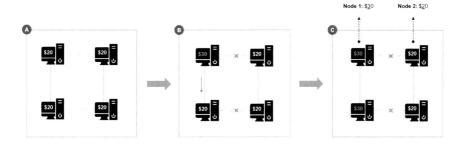

Fig. 3.2 Partition-tolerant and available, but not consistent

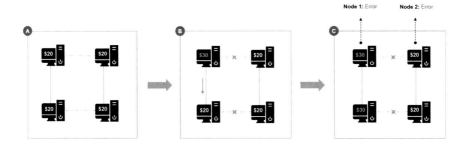

Fig. 3.3 Partition-tolerant and consistent, but not available

Scenario 3: Consistent and available, but not partition-tolerant

If we require that nodes be both consistent and available, we assume that partition tolerance is sacrificed, as in Fig. 3.4. However, if we were to introduce a partition to this scenario, it would automatically be transformed into one of the first two examples, thereby sacrificing either availability or consistency.

Rather than thinking of the CAP dimensions as binary yes/no categories, they are best viewed as lying on a triangle, where each corner represents perfect adherence to C, A, or P: Distributed database systems are points within that triangle, the positions of which illustrate how faithfully each aspect is adhered to.

A non-distributed and centralized database usually lies on the C-A edge, as partition tolerance is not required. As such, non-distributed databases can realize both consistency and availability simultaneously and are unconcerned with failing nodes or partition tolerance. Availability cannot be guaranteed if one connects to a regular database over the internet.

According to the CAP theorem, a system must always compromise. Because any production-ready system—that is, any system that is used for real applications— assumes some degree of partition tolerance, the question becomes more one of availability versus consistency, rather than a trilemma: Is it preferable to have a

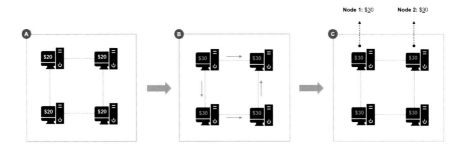

Fig. 3.4 Consistent and available, but not partition-tolerant

system return potentially outdated values, or no values at all? This question takes us to ancient Byzantium.

3.3   Byzantine Fault

3.3.1   Background

In the context of traditional computer science, Byzantine fault describes the condition of a distributed computer system in which components can fail, and information regarding component failure is incomplete [4].

In a Byzantine fault, a component like a server can appear to failure-detection systems as both failed and functioning, thus presenting different symptoms to different observers. It is difficult for the other components to declare it failed and shut it out of the network because they first have to reach a consensus regarding whether the component has failed in the first place.

The first comprehensive solution to this quandary was presented in 1999 by Miguel Castro and Barbara Liskov, when they introduced the "Practical Byzantine Fault Tolerance" (PBFT) algorithm [5]. We review this algorithm in more detail in Sect. 3.4.6, but let us first outline the basic setup of the Byzantine Fault problem using the Byzantine Generals example.

3.3.2   Byzantine Generals' Problem

The term "Byzantine Fault" originates from an allegory, the "Byzantine generals' problem," (Fig. 3.5) wherein actors must agree on a concerted strategy to avoid catastrophic failure, but some of the actors are inherently unreliable [6].

The generals' problem applies to situations involving digital money in the absence of a trusted third party. How can you be sure that a participant in a network does not send more money than he owns and that he does not send the same digital token multiple times? This is the "double-spending" problem that we have encountered before and is one of several known scam scenarios in a cryptocurrency.

Mathematicians and computer scientists use the Byzantine generals' problem as a thought experiment to explore the underlying conundrum of how to reach consensus among parties (i.e., components in a distributed system) regarding which components have been compromised (i.e., have failed) and where there is imperfect information on whether a party has been compromised (i.e., when a component has failed).

The starting point of the Byzantine generals' problem is that a group of Byzantine generals plan to assault a city surrounded by the generals and their troops. The generals must somehow ensure that all their troops attack at the same time or the plan will fail, as the city cannot be conquered if even a single general fails to attack.

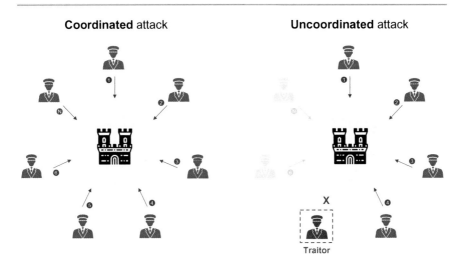

Fig. 3.5 Attack scenarios in the Byzantine generals' problem

The absence of email, text messaging, and instant messaging services in ancient Byzantium requires that generals communicate through messengers. However, there may be traitors among them who can thwart the plan by reporting false messages to the messengers and withdrawing instead of attacking. Therefore, the Byzantine generals' problem is a problem of trust and consensus-building.

3.3.3 An Example

Consider again the story of the Byzantine empire, but now allow each commander ten minutes to create a message—that is, compose it and seal it with his royal emblem. The general must also attach the entire history of previously received and sent messages.

Commander A sends a message to commander B that says, "A orders ATTACK at 4 a.m."

Ten minutes later, commander B sends a message to commander C that says, "B orders ATTACK at 4 a.m." and attaches the initial received message, "A orders ATTACK at 4 a.m."

C receives the message, but C is a traitor, so C changes the message to "C orders ATTACK at 3 a.m." and changes the messages from A and B to agree with his message, a process that requires 30–10 minutes for each message he sends

D will then receive one of the following sets of messages from C:

1. After 10 minutes, D receives: "C orders ATTACK at 3 a.m. | B orders ATTACK at 4 a.m. | A orders ATTACK at 4 a.m." Since the messages are

contradictory, D will discard C's letter and, realizing that C is corrupt, will send messages to A and B to inform them.

2. After 30 minutes, D receives: "C orders ATTACK at 3 a.m. | B orders ATTACK at 3 a.m. | A orders ATTACK at 3 a.m." Since the message was received after 30 minutes instead of 10 minutes, D realizes that C is corrupt.

The only way for C to go on with the ruse is to prepare all three messages in 10 minutes, which is practically impossible, given the work required to compose and seal them.

Now, what happens if C has extra help so he can compose and seal the three messages in parallel? In the Bitcoin equivalent, this is when hacks happen, as Bitcoin's Proof of Work (PoW) mechanism does not safeguard against hacks but only minimizes the chance of their occurrence by creating greater financial incentives for network participants to comply with the rules of the system than to break them.

The underlying assumption here is that more than half of all generals (or miners) are honest actors; if more than half are malicious and they collude, then they can make any honest actor *seem* dishonest simply by the power of their majority vote.

Such is the case in any redundant system. Another good example is the three primary flight computers (PFCs) system on modern aircraft: If two of these primary computers give the same faulty result and one gives a correct result, then the faulty result is assumed to be right, and the correct result is assumed to be wrong [7].

In practice, malicious actors usually want to increase their gains, but the lack of alignment between their individual interests prevents their colluding. In the Bitcoin network, more than half of the participating network nodes must agree for the network state to be changed, so if a lesser group of nodes colludes, or the messages they transmit are corrupt, the network will remain unaffected and resist the attack.

Thus, the second important function of a consensus algorithm is reaching consensus even when faced with faulty or malicious participants and communication paths.

3.4 Common Consensus Protocols

The blockchain protocol provides a highly effective approach to running decentralized exchanges. Changes to the state of the system by these platforms rely on the underlying consensus mechanism, which empowers the system to operate reliably, independent of the participating nodes. The rest of this chapter describes the most commonly used consensus mechanisms; for each of the protocols, we provide a brief explanation of how they work, consider their pros and cons, and review a real-world example of their implementation.

3.4.1 Proof of Work (PoW)

Principle: the more computing effort a node expends, the higher the chances that it will generate blocks.

The PoW consensus algorithm involves solving a computationally expensive calculation to add new blocks to the Bitcoin blockchain. This process is known colloquially as mining, and the nodes in the network that engage in mining are known as miners. The incentive for mining transactions lies in economic payoffs, since competing miners are rewarded with bitcoins (12.5 bitcoins as of the writing of this book), as well as transaction fees of (usually) approximately 0.20 USD for each transaction in the block that they complete and that the blockchain network accepts and appends.

How It Works

To attach new blocks to the blockchain, a node must solve a math problem using trial and error. The first participant to find a solution can distribute that solution and the block's entries to the network so other participants can build on the block and attach another block with new entries (Fig. 3.6). Providing the PoW is highly time-consuming, whereas validation by other participants is relatively quick and uncomplicated, so mutual trust among the participants is not necessary.

Real-World Usage

Consider the following example: Opening a numeric combination lock without knowing the correct combination is challenging, and the only approach to guessing the correct combination is by trial and error. However, once correctly guessed, the combination is easy to validate: Enter the combination and see if the lock opens.

Similarly, a bitcoin miner is required to produce a number (nonce) that will result in an acceptable hash for the block. This, too, is challenging, since the only way to produce such a number (nonce) is by guessing. However, once produced, the nonce can be validated easily by determining whether the number (nonce) provided by the miner results in an acceptable hash that fulfills the requirements the system sets forth.

A blockchain that is secured by the PoW mechanism is the most difficult to manipulate, given the prohibitive amount of computing power required: The PoW

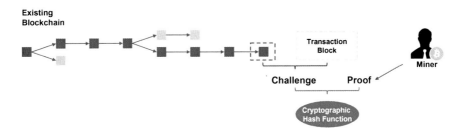

Fig. 3.6 Inner workings of the PoW mechanism

consensus mechanism requires significant energy to run, and the amount of computing power deployed by a node is directly proportional to the number of blocks that the node will solve and be rewarded for. As a result, mining power is concentrated in countries where electricity is relatively cheap, such as in the mountains of Sichuan, where abundant hydroelectric power results in the cheapest electricity prices anywhere in the world.

PoW has a high level of latency when it comes to transaction validation: it takes approximately 30 minutes (i.e., three consecutive blocks) from the time a payment instruction is sent to the time the payment originator can be sure that the transaction has been irreversibly made. This amount of time is long, especially compared to regular credit card transactions. Furthermore, PoW is susceptible to the 51% attack, which, as you recall, refers to an attack on a blockchain by a group of miners that control more than half of the network's computing power and can use it to change the blockchain's state by collectively altering enforcement of the ledger rules.

3.4.2 Proof of Stake (PoS)

Principle: The higher the stakes of validating a node in the network, the greater the chances and the legitimacy of validating blocks.

With PoS, the nodes act as validators. Rather than mining the blockchain by calculating hashes as in PoW, the validators confirm the transactions to earn a transaction fee. No traditional computing-based mining is required; all coins exist from day one.

The specific implementation of PoS can vary depending on the use case and software design. Unlike the PoW consensus regime, the PoS algorithm does not depend on expensive computational resources.

How It Works

In practice, nodes are randomly selected to validate blocks. The probability that a node will be selected depends on the number of coins that it currently holds. Validators must make a security deposit (stake); the probability of generating the next block increases with the amount of the stake: If node A stakes two coins and node B stakes one coin, node A is twice as likely to validate the next block of transactions. The validators are randomly selected, so it is not clear in advance from where the next block will come. After the selection and validation process, the general user community votes on whether to add the block.

Real-World Use

Ethereum still uses PoW but will switch to PoS in the next development phase. At first glance, PoS may not seem appealing, as those who hold the most money already, rather than those who provide the most work, are the most likely to create the next block. However, this switch will reduce the amount of electricity Ethereum requires to reach agreement on the state of transactions and contracts on the network. Furthermore, PoS-based networks are immune to malicious actors' deriving enough value from a costly attack on the network since the stake is the currency itself; the attacker would have to control more than half of the total currency in circulation to launch a successful attack.

With Ethereum's PoS implementation, Casper, the validator (i.e., the counterpart to the miner) produces the blocks [8]. If a block is successfully added to the blockchain, the validators are rewarded with ether.

Basic PoS algorithms face the Nothing-at-Stake problem, which arises because there are no direct costs for participating in the mining process. This problem impacts PoS implementations that do not provide concrete incentives for voting on the correct block: Since participants do not have to invest a currency stake to partake and nodes can vote on multiple blocks simultaneously, they can effectively support multiple forks and maximize the chances of winning a reward.

Another dimension to this problem is a malicious actor whose utility preferences are not a function of economic value but of ideology. Such a malicious actor may not care about the economic costs if he is ideologically motivated to corrupt the network, such as may be the case with state-sponsored interference.

To prevent validators from creating multiple blocks and claiming the transaction fee for each (the Nothing-at-Stake problem), the payout is tied to the process of adding the new block to the existing chain. If a block is created but not added to the blockchain, the validator loses the reward that would otherwise have been distributed for a newly added block. Because of this mechanism, manipulated blocks lose their appeal.

3.4.3   Proof of Capacity/Proof of Space

Principle: The more storage capacity a node expends, the greater the chance it will have to generate new blocks and be rewarded.

PoC is a way to prove that one has a legitimate interest in a service (e.g., a blockchain) by allocating disk space to solve a challenge presented by the service provider. PoC is a resource-friendly alternative to PoW because of the Miners for the PoC mechanism, which, as its name implies, require miners to prove their commitment by staking storage space (i.e., disk capacity), rather than computing capacity. The following example provides a simplified use case for PoC.

A provider of free mail accounts could reduce the number of fake accounts created by demanding a certain amount of hard disk space, which could be easily checked by copying a large file to it. For a normal user, 100 GB of pre-occupied system capacity is unlikely to become an issue, but for a spammer who needs this space $\times 100$, the undertaking is less feasible.

How It Works

PoC revolves around a process called plotting, which uses a relatively slow hashing algorithm called Shabal [9]. Plotting here refers to the pre-computing and storing of solutions to problems before the actual mining process starts. During the mining

Nonce

Scoop 0		Scoop 1		Scoop 2		...	Scoop 4095	
Hash #0	Hash #1	Hash #2	Hash #3	Hash #4	Hash #5		Hash #8190	Hash #8191

Fig. 3.7 Anatomy of a nonce in PoC

itself, the system protocol will ask the nodes for solutions, and the user with the largest hard drive capacity will be able to store the most solutions.

Shabal is different from the PoW SHA algorithm, where block solutions are calculated in real time. Since the Shabal hashes are difficult to calculate, and the block times are shorter (e.g., an average of 1 block every 4 minutes), the users compute and store the hashes ahead of time. Ultimately, the greater the number of available solutions, the greater a participant's chance of having the solution for the most recent puzzle first.

When creating a plot file, users create nonces (Sect. 1.4.2) through repeated hashing of data, including a user's account ID. The more disk space is allocated to plotting, the more nonces can be stored. One nonce will eventually contain 8,192 hashes (Fig. 3.7) organized in pairs known as scoops. Every scoop is assigned a number from 0 to 4095.

Real-World Use

A node calculates a scoop number between 0 and 4095 as part of the mining process. Once a number (e.g., 42) is determined, the miner selects scoop 42 of nonce 1 and uses that scoop data to derive a random point in time, referred to as the "deadline" (Fig. 3.7). The miner then repeats this process for all nonces in the plot file. After calculating all the deadlines, the miner chooses the shortest deadline, which is the number of seconds that elapsed between the forging of blocks. If no one else has forged a block after this time has passed, the miner can forge a block and claim the block reward.

PoC solves the energy-related problem of the classic PoW algorithms because it reduces energy consumption, given the nature of the resource staked (i.e., disk space).

3.4.4 Delegated Proof of Stake (DPoS)

Principle: The higher the stake of a validating node in the network, the more votes it can delegate to another trusted node to perform the validation.

DPoS is a fast-consensus mechanism that is best known for its implementation in EOS, an ERC-20 token. In this context, "fast" refers to the shorter block-confirmation times. DPoS is frequently referred to as digital or representative democracy because of its stake-weighted voting system.

DPoS is based on the concept of the "proof of stake." The actors in a DPoS system are called voters, witnesses, and delegates. In this process of technology-enabled democracy, protecting the network relies on a voting and election process.

How It Works

In DPoS, participants receive one vote for possessing a token. The users of a DPoS-based blockchain vote for "witnesses" and "delegates" by placing their tokens on individual candidates. This process differs from the PoS model, where anyone who holds tokens in a wallet can, in principle, qualify as a validator for a new block.

Witnesses in the network are responsible for its security and can validate new blocks. Only a subset of the witnesses selected is paid for their work, and of this subset, an even smaller subset receives regular (i.e., cyclical) income for its efforts. Because the electoral system runs continuously, those who neglect their work or act fraudulently can be voted off at any time, which motivates the witnesses to do their work conscientiously.

In addition to the witnesses, the community also elects delegates, who are akin to legislators who help guide and regulate the system's operations. They are responsible for maintaining the network, its governance, and the blockchain's performance but, unlike witnesses, cannot validate transactions. Delegates also can submit proposals to change the block sizes or the witness fees, which are subsequently voted on.

Real-World Use

Well-known examples of cryptocurrencies that use DPoS include Lisk, EOS, and BitShares.

3.4.5 Proof of Authority (PoA)

Principle: A select set of N established participants hold elevated authority in the blockchain; any participant with such authority can propose the next block, and if a subset of participants signs the block, it is added to the blockchain.

Unlike all the other consensus mechanisms, PoA is considered to be non-democratic and can be used for permissioned ledgers. The mechanism centers on the use of "authorities," which are designated nodes that can create new blocks and secure the ledger. The specific implementation rules can vary but, overall, the ledger of a PoA system requires a sign-off by a subset of authorities (i.e., m out of all N authorities) for a new block to be created.

How It Works

PoA is comparable to PoS, but instead of a resource stake, the nodes stake their identities for the right to create a new block. Each authoritative node must voluntarily disclose its pseudonymous identity in the form of its public key. The identity stake can serve as a great equalizer, as participants whose identities and, thus, reputations are at stake, are incented to preserve the network, while malicious actors are easily identified.

The following conditions must be met for PoA to function in a real-world setting:

- *Identity verification*: The methods for verifying identities and preventing subversion by malicious actors must be standardized and robust.
- *Staking eligibility*: The right to be a validator must be difficult to obtain.
- *Authority establishment*: A consistent procedure ensures that all nodes comprehend the process and trust its integrity.

The best-known examples of the use of a PoA consensus mechanism today are the two Ethereum test-nets, Kovan and Rinkeby.

3.4.6 Practical Byzantine Fault Tolerance (PBFT)

Principle: Consensus by a two-thirds supermajority vote (e.g., two vs. one).

In any fault-tolerant system, messages may be subject to loss, corruption, a high level of latency, and repetition. In addition, the transmission order may not match the order in which the message was received. Node activities are also unpredictable, as nodes can enter or leave the network at any time or may lose information, falsify it, or simply stop working. Practical Byzantine Fault Tolerance (PBFT) provides a fault tolerance of $f = \lfloor(n - 1)/3\rfloor$ for a consensus system comprised of n nodes. A fault tolerance capacity of 1/3 provides security and is suitable for any network environment.

How It Works

The PBFT algorithm ensures security and ease of use. With no more than $\lfloor(n - 1)/3\rfloor$ erroneous nodes in consensus, where $n = |R|$, with n the number of nodes involved in consensus-building, and R the set of consensus nodes, the system's functionality and stability are guaranteed. Given $f = \lfloor(n - 1)/3\rfloor$, f represents the maximum number of failed nodes allowed in the system.

The entire blockchain is managed by bookkeeping nodes, while ordinary nodes are not involved in consensus-building. All consensus (i.e., bookkeeping) nodes must maintain a log file to record the current consensus status. The record used for consensus from beginning to end is called a view; if no consensus can be reached in the current view, a change of the view is required.

Technical Explanation

We identify each view with a natural number v, starting at 0, which can increase until a state of consensus is reached; we also identify each consensus node with a number starting at 0 but ending with $n - 1$. For each round of consensus-finding, one node will play "house speaker," while other nodes will play "congresspersons."

The number of the speaker p is determined by the following algorithm: Given the current block height h, then $p = (h - v) mod\ n$, so the range for p is $0 \leq p < n$.

Each round of consensus generates a new block of at least $n - f$ signatures from bookkeeping nodes. When a block is created, a new round of consensus-building is started that resets $v = 0$.

3.4.7 Proof of Elapsed Time (PoET)

Principle: A trusted hardware chip that first randomly selects a time duration and then waits until the selected time has elapsed.

In PoW, PoC, PoS, and DPoS, democratization of the consensus participants is hindered by the fact that mining power is distributed based on expendable capital (e.g., either an investment in mining hardware or a cryptocurrency capital stake). PoET aims to provide a more democratic consensus by allowing each participant a fair degree of participation. Currently, only PoET enables a "one CPU, one vote" implementation that is independent of computing power or other resource expenditures. Such a scheme is achieved primarily by providing a trusted execution environment (TEE), which is a secured enclave within the CPU that is used to protect highly sensitive information, such as encryption keys. In practice, a modern CPU enclave is nearly impossible to hack, not only because of the intractably small physical scale, on the order of 10 nm (which is observable only with an electron microscope), but also because they use manufacturer-attested cryptographic keys that are embedded within the hardware itself.

How It Works

In PoET, every participant randomly selects a time duration and then waits for that duration to elapse (hold-up time). Intel Software Guard Extensions (SGX) is an example of a hardware-based implementation of security-related instruction codes. The participant with the shortest hold-up time proposes the next block and must provide a signature proving that the hold-up time was randomly selected and that the participant waited for that hold-up time to elapse.

All network nodes can easily validate the claim for a new block by using a mathematical proof provided by the claiming node's TEE. The node that suggests the new block must prove that it had the shortest wait time of all the participating nodes and that it has waited for the amount of time designated by the protocol before starting the mining of the subsequent block.

The randomness of the waiting times for each node ensures the random distribution of the leader role. However, a weakness of the PoET consensus mechanism is that it requires specialized hardware, along with the associated cost and set-up complexity.

3.4.8   Other Mechanisms

New protocols offer both advantages and disadvantages and are constantly being developed and improved upon. These models for finding consensus are usually implemented on individual and smaller projects, but they deserve a mention.

One is a mixture of PoW and PoS with Proof of Activity. In this scenario, blocks are generated without transactions via PoW, and who completes the block is determined via PoS. Blockchain adds an extra level of decentralization to this process, but this mixture combines the potential problems of PoW (power consumption) and PoS (Nothing at Stake).

Another conceptual system, Proof of Burn, is sometimes mentioned but is not used in practice. Here, the system's coins or another cryptocurrency are destroyed by sending them to an address that collects coins but cannot return them. As is the case with PoS, spending more money increases the chances of creating blocks and being rewarded.

Regardless of the details of the mechanism at play, the core directive is the same: Hurdles are set up through consensus algorithms to prevent manipulation and duplication of rewards/transaction fees by miners/validators.

When the application's architect selects a consensus mechanism and platform for an application, she should consider the relationships between participants, as well as the functional and non-functional aspects of the application. The functional aspects of a blockchain application that is supported by a consensus mechanism can include the type of transaction, transaction time, transaction throughput, node/network availability, transaction finality, and the ability to roll back transactions. Non-functional aspects of a blockchain application include participant identity, participant trust, incentive alignment, and the regulatory environment. An up-to-date overview of this evolving landscape is critical to ensuring a reasoned choice of consensus models.

3.5   Exercise

3.5.1   Introduction

After launching a Proof-of-Work (PoW) blockchain as part of the exercise in Chap. 1 and conducting a first transaction in Chap. 2, we proceed to launching a Proof-of-Authority (PoA) blockchain.

The difference between the two consensus mechanisms is that, with PoW, the control of the network lies with the party that controls the most computing power, while with PoA, the control of the network is pre-assigned to specific parties.

3.5.2 Set up PoA Genesis Block

Next, we will set up a Proof-of-Authority (PoA)-based blockchain. If you need help re-connecting or setting-up your docker instance, refer to 2.6.2a and 2.6.2b.

In your docker instance, navigate to the test1 folder that you created in Chap. 1. Before we continue, we will create separate accounts, as well as a separate base directory (node_poa) for our PoA-based exercise.

To create a new Ethereum account on your local instance, use the following command. (The node_poa folder contains the both the databases and keystore for the new PoA-based network.)

```
geth account new --datadir node_poa
```

As before, you will be prompted to specify a passphrase. For now, you can press the enter key twice to skip this step, as we will not be using a password.

```
Your new account is locked with a password. Please give a password.
Do not forget this password.
Passphrase:
Repeat passphrase:
```

Now you will see your newly created Ethereum address displayed in the command line; it should look something like this:

```
Address: {6287b3be866b1d2615337f9b3025f1ceaaef34ed}
```

In the *test1* folder use the puppeth command to configure and launch a private PoA network on your simulated machine by following the steps below:

```
> puppeth
```

First, you will be prompted to specify an Ethereum network name, so type *node_pow*.

```
Please specify a network name to administer (no spaces or hyphens, please)
> node_poa
```

Then you will be asked to select an action. Choose 2 to configure a new genesis.

```
What would you like to do? (default = stats)
 1. Show network stats
 2. Configure new genesis
 3. Track new remote server
 4. Deploy network components
> 2
```

Next comes a prompt to specify what you want to do. Choose 1 to create a new genesis block from scratch.

```
What would you like to do? (default = create)
 1. Create new genesis block from scratch
 2. Import already existing genesis
 > 1
```

Next, you will be prompted to select a consensus algorithm. Choose 2 to use proof-of-authority.

```
Which consensus engine to use? (default = clique)
 1. Ethash - proof-of-work
 2. Clique - proof-of-authority
 > 2
```

With a PoA-based network, you can select how long it will take to mine each block. For now, you can just choose the default of 15 seconds:

```
How many seconds should blocks take? (default = 15)
 > 15
```

Now a prompt asks you to specify which accounts can seal. This "sealing" refers to the creation of new blocks. An alternative way of asking this question would be to ask which accounts should be endowed with authority for this PoA blockchain:

```
Which accounts are allowed to seal? (mandatory at least one)
 > 0x6287b3be866b1d2615337f9b3025f1ceaaef34ed
```

Next comes a prompt to specify pre-funded accounts. You can pre-fund the same accounts as well be providing it.

```
Which accounts should be pre-funded? (advisable at least one)
 > 0x6287b3be866b1d2615337f9b3025f1ceaaef34ed
```

You will now be prompted regarding whether you want to pre-fund your initial address with 1 wei. Type "yes" and press enter to pre-fund the address.

```
Should the precompile-addresses (0x1 .. 0xff) be pre-funded with 1 wei? (advisable yes)
 > yes
```

Next, you will be prompted to specify a network identifier. Type "101" and press enter:

```
Specify your chain/network ID if you want an explicit one (default = random)
 > 101
```

Then you will be asked to select an action. Choose 2 to manage the existing genesis.

```
What would you like to do? (default = stats)
  1. Show network stats
  2. Manage existing genesis
  3. Track new remote server
  4. Deploy network components
> 2
```

The next prompt asks you to select an action. Choose 2 to export the genesis.

```
  1. Modify existing fork rules
  2. Export genesis configuration
  3. Remove genesis configuration
> 2
```

You will now be prompted to select a folder into which to save the genesis specs. Press enter to select the default (current) folder.

```
Which folder to save the genesis specs into? (default = current)
  Will create node_poa.json, node_poa-aleth.json, node_poa-harmony.json,node_poa-parity.json
```

Finally, you will be asked to select an action. Press the key combination control + c to exit geth; after that, you should again see the root@… command prompt.

```
What would you like to do? (default = stats)
  1. Show network stats
  2. Manage existing genesis
  3. Track new remote server
  4. Deploy network components
> ^C
```

3.5.3 Create a PoA Network

In your test1 directory on your docker instance, use the `geth` command to start a new PoA network using the configured genesis that you just created:

```
geth init node_poa.json --datadir node_poa
```

Next, use `geth` to initiate the mining process, just as you did before:

```
geth --verbosity 2 console --datadir node_poa --nousb
```

Also as before, you can start the mining process using the `miner.start()` command:

```
miner.start()
null
> WARN [10-29|17:26:40.840] Block sealing failed     err="authentication needed: password or unlock"
```

Now, since we are operating in the PoA-based world, you will notice that you cannot just start the mining process like you did in a PoW-based setup using the miner.start() command because your account is locked, and the ability to mine is tied to your account rights.

```
> personal.unlockAccount(personal.listAccounts[0]);
Unlock account 0x6287b3be866b1d2615337f9b3025f1ceaaef34ed
Passphrase:
true
```

You must first unlock your (only) personal account with PoA mining rights:

```
miner.start()
nuell
```

After this step, you should be able to initiate the mining process:

```
miner.start()
null
```

As before, you can validate your success using the `eth.mining` command:

```
eth.mining
true
```

Congratulations! you have successfully launched your own PoA blockchain network and initiated the mining process!

References

1. Attaran M (2019) Applications of blockchain technology in business: challenges and opportunities. Springer Nature, Bakersfield
2. Narayanan A, Bonneau J, Felten E et al (2016) Bitcoin and cryptocurrency technologies: a comprehensive introduction. Princeton University Press, Princeton
3. Borah S, Ballas V, Polkowski Z (2020) Advances in data science and management. In: Proceedings of ICDSM 2019. Springer, Singapore
4. Zhao W (2014) Building dependable distributed systems. Wiley, Beverly
5. Raj K (2019) Foundations of blockchain: the pathway to cryptocurrencies and decentralized blockchain applications. Packt Publishing, Birmingham
6. Kelly B (2015) The bitcoin big bang: how alternative currencies are about to change the world. Wiley, Hoboken

7. Yeh YC (1996) Triple-triple redundant 777 primary fight computer
8. Wu X (2019) Learn ethereum: build your own decentralized applications with ethereum and smart contracts. Packt, Birmingham
9. Biryukov A, Gong G, Stinson D (2011) Selected areas in cryptography. In: 17th international workshop, SAC 2010. Springer, Heidelberg

Smart Contracts

4

4.1 Introduction

One of the most exciting topics to emerge in the blockchain ecosystem is the smart contract. A smart contract is a computer program whose code is stored in a distributed blockchain structure and that directly controls digital assets without relying on a third-party intermediary. (See Fig. 4.1.) The program determines autonomously whether contract conditions were met by retrieving external data using pre-defined application programming interfaces (APIs) as a source, and executes a contract (e.g., a value transfer) accordingly. Smart contracts can facilitate or even fully automate insurance processes, financial instruments, and legal processes that are currently heavily paper-based, long-winded, and expensive.

The Ethereum smart contract platform has gained the most momentum so far. The Ethereum project runs a public blockchain platform that is similar to but separate from the Bitcoin blockchain, with extensive, Turing-complete smart-contract functionality [1]. (See Sect. 4.6 for details on Turing completeness.) Several technology companies, including IBM, have run pilot projects using the Ethereum infrastructure. Microsoft, for instance, announced its support for Ethereum on its Azure infrastructure-as-a-service (IaaS) platform as early as 2015. The Ethereum system itself provides a decentralized virtual machine that can execute smart contracts using a cryptocurrency called Ether (ETH), and a construct called Gas to pay for computing and storage infrastructure [2].

Most of today's smart contracts are coded manually and include only a description of the contract's conditions, scenarios, and outcomes. However, this process could be simplified, allowing smart contracts to be standardized across industries and adjusted for or tailored to certain uses. Of course, not all aspects of a smart contract have to be fully automated: The smart contract code can account for special scenarios under which the contract provides a mediator with mitigation

© Springer Nature Switzerland AG 2020

D. Hellwig et al., *Build Your Own Blockchain*, Management for Professionals,

https://doi.org/10.1007/978-3-030-40142-9_4

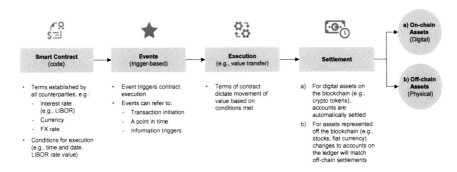

Fig. 4.1 Smart contract flow diagram

authority over the outcome (e.g., the funds that are to be transferred). Customers could then use blockchain-enabled smart contracts without concerning themselves with the elements of the underlying technology.

The piggy bank example shown in Fig. 4.2 is a basic working example of a smart contract code that can be deployed on the Ethereum blockchain as it is. The example shows how to generate a contract that allows any user to deposit any amount but only the owner of the contract to take the money out (after a specified amount has been accumulated—1 ETH in this example).

```solidity
pragma solidity ^0.5.1;

contract Piggybank                              # Piggybank contract that allows
{                                                 spending if savings are > 1 ETH

    address payable public owner;               # Contract owner

    constructor() public
    {                                           # Creation of contract
        owner = msg.sender;
    }

    function() payable external
    {                                           # Saving funds
    }

    function spend() public
    {                                           # Return all savings to the
        require(msg.sender == owner);             contract owner
        require(address(this).balance >= 1 ether);
        owner.transfer(address(this).balance);
    }

}
```

Fig. 4.2 Piggy bank example

This chapter uses the Ethereum ecosystem and its primary programming language, Solidity, to illustrate how smart contracts operate and to outline the major challenges that face this technology today. We introduce two additional concepts: Oracles, which provide the technical means for data exchanges with off-chain data providers (e.g., banks, weather stations) and decentralized applications, or dApps, which are fully operational computer programs that run autonomously on the blockchain. The chapter concludes with a perspective on the current legal realm of smart contracts and other challenges related to their execution.

4.2 Ethereum—An Alternative to Bitcoin

4.2.1 Introduction

Ethereum was conceived in 2013 by Vitalik Buterin, a Canadian Bitcoin programmer, who started operations in 2015. Ethereum should be distinguished from Ethereum Classic (ETC), from which it split off in 2016 after a dispute among the developers concerning the decentralized autonomous organization (DAO) project. (See Sect. 4.3.) Since its introduction, Ethereum has become popular with maintainers and users alike: As of 2019, its blockchain is the second largest in terms of stored data (>244 GB), superseded only by the original Bitcoin blockchain ($\sim$258 GB).

The official documentation of Ethereum states that "Ethereum is an open blockchain platform that lets anyone build and use decentralized applications that run on blockchain technology." As such, the Ethereum blockchain platform's focus is on facilitating scripting functionality, or smart contracts, which are run by the nodes in the network [3]. The network nodes provide the computing and storage resources as well; as a result, and unlike the Bitcoin blockchain, Ethereum not only tracks but also programs transactions. Thus, Ethereum is a blockchain-based network like Bitcoin that provides smart contract functionality in addition to enabling pure monetary transactions. Operated by a non-profit foundation, Ethereum has grown to be the largest platform for smart contracts and, as of 2019, also has the largest developer community by far.

By extending the concept of Bitcoin to include dynamic elements in the blockchain, Ethereum aims to become the foundation of the whole blockchain ecology. Indeed, the vast majority of blockchain projects today do not have their own blockchain but use Ethereum's blockchain as a basis. The Ethereum project also has a separate cryptocurrency called Ether (ETH).

4.2.2 Ethereum Versus Bitcoin Applications

Before Ethereum, Bitcoin supported a set of basic instructions called operation codes (opcodes), which form the Bitcoin scripting language [3]. Using these instructions, one can store data and send or receive bitcoins. The most frequently used scripts are a signature script (abbreviated `scriptSig`) and a pubkey script (abbreviated `scriptPubKey`). A pubkey script is composed of the opcodes `OP_DUP OP_HASH160OP_EQUALVERIFY` and `OP_CHECKSIG`, while a signature script simply requires a signature (usually the owner's signature, which can be generated only with the owner's private key). More complex scripts can contain many instructions and conditions, such as freezing funds until a certain time in the future, requiring multiple signatures for spending funds, and even gambling.

For example, in the Bitcoin ecosystem, a transmitter can define the conditions under which the receiver can send a balance (i.e., the unspent transaction output (UTXO) from a previous transaction). (Remember, in the Bitcoin realm, there are no account balances, but only UTXOs from previous transactions.) The rationale for implementing this functionality in the Bitcoin protocol was to increase flexibility in dealing with bitcoins without constantly having to update the node software; the user specifies a script to execute in a transaction, and the miner executes it.

Figure 4.3 shows a working example of a script that allows only the amount deposited at the specified address to be spent and only after a given date (here, 1668165071, which is the Unix epoch time, Friday, 2022-11-11 11:11:11 UTC).

Bitcoin is based on a Forth-like, stack-based scripting language and, unlike Ethereum, does not offer a Turing-complete instruction set—see Sect. 4.6—because,

```
1668165071                     # Push date value on top of the stack (Unix time),

OP_CHECKLOCKTIMEVERIFY         # If current time is before the top of the stack (above date), stop.

OP_DROP                        # Pop the top of the stack (above date).

OP_DUP                         # Duplicate the top of the stack (the senderis public key).

OP_HASH160                     # Hash (with RIPEMD160) the senderis public key on top of the stack
                               and replace the top of the stack.

9c1185a5c5e9fc546128...        # Push value on top of the stack (script unlock hash).

OP_EQUALVERIFY                 # Verify that the two top stack items are equal by comparing senderis
                               public key hash and scripting unlock hash to verify that the sender
                               owns funds.

OP_CHECKSIG                    # Check that the senderis public key verifies against the script
                               signature (verifies the scriptis integrity).
```

Fig. 4.3 Bitcoin-based contract code

with a full Turing instruction set, it is virtually impossible to know in advance whether the running process will also be terminated. In practice, the process can get caught in an endless loop. Consider the following instructions that will produce an infinite loop:

Variable x has value 2. Repeat the statement x = x – 0 until x takes the value of 1.

We can subtract 0 from 2 an infinite number of times, and the result will never be 1, so the program gets hung up. In this example, the error is easy to recognize, but it is impossible to know whether loops with a certain level of complexity will ever terminate because of the halting problem. The halting problem, as Alan Turing proved in 1936, is that no algorithm can decide whether a non-trivial program ever terminates [4].

The halting problem applies only to non-trivial programs, as trivial programs do not have to be reviewed. When writing a program to determine whether another program terminates, the new program will naturally be more complex than the program to be analyzed. The halting problem is closely related to Kurt Gödel's incompleteness theorem, published in 1931, which shows that a non-trivial axiomatic system cannot demonstrate its consistency [5].

The implications of this setup are profound for the creation of smart contracts, as a user could purposely write malicious code to so that, if the miners run a program that gets stuck in a loop, the software crashes, paralyzing the network. This threat has prompted researchers to consider less powerful and safer languages because the code always terminates. The drawback is that certain logic cannot be formulated, and the code can easily become so long that the codebase becomes unmanageable.

Next, we will see how Ethereum addresses the challenge of infinitely running code for its smart contract platform.

4.2.3 Ethereum Approach

While the functionalities of the Ethereum blockchain resemble Bitcoin's, Ethereum stands out in that it allows for a much more complex set of instructions and relies on the Gas concept to charge users for executing code. (See Sect. 4.2.4.)

Because of its more advanced instruction set, the Ethereum blockchain enables smart contracts, computer programs that run as decentralized applications (dApps) in a virtual runtime environment called the Ethereum Virtual Machine (EVM). The EVM is a simulated computer that can execute a set of instructions that are translated into the underlying machine code and then run on the non-virtual computer hardware provided by the miners.

Therefore, the blockchain is no longer a mere list of transactions, as it also guarantees the authenticity and execution correctness of entire automatically running computer programs. Therefore, dApps and smart contracts work like programs that are triggered by an event like a transaction in Ether, to perform predefined actions automatically.

4.2.4   Gas

The developers of the EVM implemented a Turing-complete instruction set-up, which is possible because every instruction that the virtual machine executes has a price. (See Fig. 4.4.) In the Ethereum ecosystem, the cost of running a smart contract code is measured in units called gas. Charging execution costs addresses the problem of infinite execution times that was outlined in Sect. 4.2.2, as any infinite loop will eventually be terminated when the contract runs out of gas.

The EVM's individual programming instructions each have their own gas cost, as depicted in Fig. 4.4, so when an originator launches a smart contract, she must always set the gas limit to indicate the maximum gas that the smart contract may consume during its execution [6].

Ideally, the program terminates before the gas limit is reached, and the originator pays exactly the gas the smart contract consumes. However, if all the gas is used up, either because the program gets stuck in a loop or the gas limit is too low, the smart contract terminates. In such cases, a correctly programmed smart contract will terminate without making any changes, while a poorly programmed smart contract may yield unexpected results, such as becoming permanently inaccessible or allowing fraudulent use.

Ethereum-based smart contracts can be thought of as transactions with extensive rules and conditions. (See Fig. 4.5 for the anatomy of an Ethereum block.)

Value	Mnemonic	Gas Used	Subset	Removed from stack	Added to stack	Notes
0x00	STOP	0	zero	0	0	Halts execution.
0x01	ADD	3	very low	2	1	Addition operation
0x02	MUL	5	low	2	1	Multiplication operation
0x03	SUB	3	very low	2	1	Subtraction operation
0x04	DIV	5	low	2	1	Integer division operation
0x05	SDIV	5	low	2	1	Signed integer division operation (truncated)
0x06	MOD	5	low	2	1	Modulo remainder operation
0x07	SMOD	5	low	2	1	Signed modulo remainder operation
0x08	ADDMOD	8	mid	3	1	Modulo addition operation
				...		

Fig. 4.4 Ethereum instructions and gas costs

Gas consumption is higher for a complex smart contract than it is for a simpler one, so the gas limit should be higher to prevent the contract from running out of gas before it fully executes all the instructions contained in the smart contract code. Gas is awarded to the miner who successfully packs the transaction into a block and executes its code.

4.2.5   The Price of Gas

In addition to the gas limit, the originator specifies the gas price for the transaction, which sets how much Ether she is willing to pay per unit of gas. Thus, a market similar to transaction costs with Bitcoin emerges, where greater payments lead to faster transaction times. If the network is busy, the average price of gas rises as miners select transactions that bring in more Ether.

The gas price is usually in the range of a billionth of an ether. A billionth (10^{-9}) of an ether is also called a gigawei (GW) or simply gwei, where 1 wei is 10^{-18} ethers.

Consider the following example: We carry out a transaction that consumes 1475 gas and set the gas price at 17 GW. Thus, if we choose a gas limit of 1475 or more, we will pay $17 \times 10^{-9} \times 1475 = 0.000025075$ ethers for the transaction. If we set the gas limit to less than 1475, the transaction will not be completed, but we will still have to pay the miner for trying to execute the transaction before running out of gas.

4.3   Solidity Programming Language

Solidity is the fourth programming language for Ethereum. As the most advanced and the first object-oriented, high-level programming language for Ethereum, it leverages a JavaScript-like syntax, which allows for modern programming constructs like abstraction, interfaces, and polymorphism (i.e., the ability to derive classes).

- **Transaction:** An Ethereum transaction can be sent from one address to another address, as in Bitcoin.

- **Contract:** A smart contract is mined when a transaction is sent to the null address; the transaction data field holds the contract code.

- **Interaction:** Users and contracts can interact with each other by sending transactions between their respective addresses.

- **Triggers:** A transaction to a smart contract can trigger a function within that contract, initiating an automated sequence.

- **Compute:** Calculations are performed by each miner, and data can be stored on the blockchain; both cost ether, measured in gas.

- **Accounts:** Ethereum's equivalent of Bitcoin's unspent transactions (UTXO) is a store of accounts (addresses) and their balances.

- **Balance:** Transactions are valid only if the sender account has sufficient balance; the sender is debited, and the receiver credited.

Fig. 4.5 Ethereum block layout

Solidity is used primarily for developing smart contracts that can be compiled into bytecode for the EVM, which are uploaded in turn to the Ethereum blockchain (e.g., through the Ethereum Geth Console). There are several methods by which to compile Solidity code, including the online compiler, the command-line Solidity compiler solc, and the compiler built into Ethereum.

4.3.1 Syntax

The Solidity syntax is based heavily on the ECMAScript syntax [7] to help web developers get started on smart contract development. However, unlike ECMA-Script, the Solidity syntax is statically typed and supports variable return values. Compared to other smart contract programming languages (LLL, Serpent, Mutan, etc.), Solidity supports complex types of variables, such as hierarchical mappings and constructors, which can also be nested, as well as an inheritance for contracts. External applications and libraries (e.g., the browser library Web3.js) can interact with Ethereum contracts via the Application Binary Interface (ABI), the specifics of which are beyond the scope of this introductory volume [8]. However, one can think about the ABI as a set of rules to which compilers and linkers adhere to compile a smart contract properly. ABIs cover multiple topics:

- **Procedures**: How should smart contract functions be translated to assembly code?
- **Function Names**: How should functions be represented to allow other smart contracts to know how to interact with them (i.e., what arguments to pass)?
- **Data Types**: What types of data can be used, and do they need to be formatted?

Solidity allows smart contracts to be uploaded to the Ethereum blockchain and to be executed by one of the network's nodes, as demonstrated with the coin toss example in the next section.

4.3.2 Coin Toss Example

A simple coin toss (heads or tails) can constitute a smart contract on Ethereum. This basic gamble can be implemented based on the ETH cryptocurrency. The game begins when two players throw a minimum currency stake into a virtual pot—that is, they send ETH to an address as defined by the contract. During its execution time, the smart contract randomly determines the winner of the coin toss (using

50:50 odds) by running a random-number generator implemented by the EVM. The contract then immediately and automatically transfers the winnings to the account of the person who won.

The *Coin* contract provides a more complex example of a smart contract written in the Solidity programming language (Fig. 4.6). In this example, two bettors can stake a pre-defined amount, and the winner is determined randomly via the smart contract based on the parity of the unpredictable block hash (i.e., whether the block hash is even or odd).

4.4   Oracles

4.4.1   Introduction

The network participants (nodes) validate and execute operations performed on the blockchain, such as smart contracts, but it is not uncommon for a smart contract to require data from external third parties. Given that blockchains cannot access data outside their networks, how is external data incorporated into the workflow? Here is where Oracles come in.

```solidity
pragma solidity ^0.5.1;

contract Coin                                          # Coin toss contract.
{                                                      Allows two bettors to bet
                                                       on a predefined amount.

    uint256 amount;
    uint256 blockNumber;                               # Contract owner
    address payable[] bettors;

    constructor(uint256 amount_) public                # Creates the contract.
    {                                                  @param amount_ the
        amount = amount_;                              bet amount, in Wei.
    }

    function bet() payable public
    {
        require(msg.value == amount);
        require(bettors.length < 2);                   # Places a bet.
        blockNumber = block.number + 1;
        bettors.push(msg.sender);
    }

    function toss()public
    {
        require(bettors.length == 2);
        require(blockNumber < block.number);           # Tosses the coin and
        uint256 winner = uint256(blockhash(block.number)) % 2;   pays the winner.
        bettors[winner].transfer(address(this).balance);
    }

}
```

Fig. 4.6 Coin toss example (solidity)

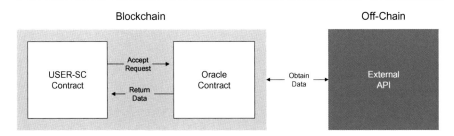

Fig. 4.7 Oracle anatomy

Oracles are agents on the blockchain that can verify events from the real world and then provide the corresponding information as data to the smart contracts (Fig. 4.7). Running on the blockchain, Oracles act as intermediaries between external data and smart contracts that also run on the blockchain [9]. Smart contracts usually specify only sequences like "If condition C has occurred, operation O will be executed." To check whether the condition has been met, smart contracts often rely on external data. One example is sensors that measure real-world phenomena. For example, if you want to implement insurance through a smart contract that pays direct compensation when certain temperatures are reached, an Oracle must provide the temperature information.

4.4.2 Smart Contract Integration

The addition of an Oracle occurs through multi-signature (MultiSig) contracts, which require that an invocation of a smart contract method be signed by multiple parties. To improve trust in the external data a smart contract that an Oracle provides and to prevent the Oracle from being compromised by one party, data can be signed by multiple parties: In the case of a stock price Oracle, one can set up MultiSig so each stock price data item must be signed by three independent parties (e.g., Bloomberg, NASDAQ, and MSNBC).

4.4.3 Oracles and Security

The basic principle of blockchain is that a consensus is reached through the involvement of multiple parties, eliminating the need to trust a single party. However, if the data is provided by a central authority like a bank, the data-providing authority must be trusted.

4.4.4 Types of Oracles

Data sources for smart contract Oracles can be classified into five types:

- **Software Oracle**: Data is available online and is, ideally, provided from multiple independent sources, has a public record history (e.g., air traffic information, meteorological data), and is signed by multiple parties.
- **Hardware Oracle**: Data is from real-world measurements like RFID sensors in a supply chain site. Challenges with this type of data source include that there is usually only one source, there is no public record history, it is signed by only one party, and transmitting the information in a secure and provably immutable way is difficult.

From a technical perspective, Oracles can also be classified by their functional setup—that is, based on data flow (inbound vs. outbound) and whether they are consensus-based or not. This delineation is not mutually exclusive, so some data can be both inbound and outbound.

- **Inbound Oracles**: These Oracles provide a smart contract with information from the outside world. For example, a buy order is set to be executed as soon as the EUR-USD exchange rate falls below a certain limit.
- **Outbound Oracles**: These Oracles enable smart contracts to send data to the outside instead of just receiving it. For example, access to an area may be granted when a payment has been made on the blockchain (e.g., via a smart lock).
- **Consensus-based Oracles**: Several Oracles are combined so one does not have to rely on a single external source. These Oracles then form a consensus to make decisions. An example is a consensus Oracle that specifies that three out of five Oracles must agree before an operation is executed. Of course, it is also possible to apply scores to individual Oracles such that a source carries more weight if it appears to be more reliable than other sources.

4.4.5 Oracle Contract Example

The *Oracle* contract provides a simple working example of an Oracle smart contract written in the Solidity programming language (Fig. 4.8). In this example, the Oracle can provide the USD-EUR foreign exchange (FX) rate to other smart contacts on a blockchain: The contact specifies the owner (i.e., a single-signature Oracle), the timestamp input (to determine when the FX rate can be returned), and the FX rate itself, which other smart contacts can access.

```
pragma solidity ^0.5.1;
```

```
contract Oracle                                    # Oracle contract.
{                                                  A single-signature inbound
                                                   Oracle for the USD-EUR
                                                   exchange rate.

    address payable public owner;                  # Oracle owner

    uint8 public decimals;                         # USD-EUR
                                                   exchange rate

    uint256 public timestamp;                      # USD-EUR exchange rate
                                                   timestamp


    constructor() public
    {
        owner = msg.sender;                        # Creates the contract
    }


                                                   # Sets the new exchange
    function set(uint8 decimals_, uint256 rate_) public    rate
    {
        require(msg.sender == owner);              * @param decimals_ the
        require(rate_ > 0);                        USD-EUR exchange rate
        decimals = decimals_;                      decimal position
        rate = rate_;
        timestamp = block.timestamp;               * @param rate_ the USD-
    }                                              EUR exchange rate


}
```

Fig. 4.8 Oracle for the USD-EUR exchange rate

4.5   Decentralized Applications (dApps)

4.5.1   Introduction

dApps, shorthand for "decentralized applications," include all applications that are based on distributed ledger technology. In the broadest sense, every cryptocurrency is a dApp, so all dApps should have certain properties:

- All data is stored and cryptographically secured in a blockchain.
- It is free, open-source software, preferably developed by an open community.
- Decisions are reached by community consensus, ideally on the blockchain itself.
- Existing or newly created tokens are used to regulate access and rewards.

If an application does not fulfill each of these requirements, it may not be strictly considered a "dApp," but this set of rules is not always adhered to.

Since dApps applications are run on Ethereum in a decentralized, consensus-based fashion, unwanted interference is virtually impossible. Only authorized parties, of which there may be none, can alter the dApp; unauthorized parties cannot secretly tamper with the application, change the code, prevent it from working, or apply censorship.

At their core, dApps enable applications to run where a centralized authority or broker need not be trusted. For example, Uber is a non-decentralized app run by the Uber corporation. Users rely on this central entity to match drivers and riders, while the company retains the profits and may arbitrarily create and apply new rules. With a dApp, on the other hand, the matching service could be provided with no central party running the service, as all logic is embedded in the code itself and may be either unalterable or altered only through a consensus mechanism.

High-profile dApps built on the Ethereum platform include:

- Augur, a Decentralized Prediction Market
  https://augur.net
- Digix, which tokenizes gold on Ethereum
  https://digix.global
- Maker, a Decentralized Autonomous Organization (DAO)
  https://makerdao.com

dApps, like all blockchain projects, have a wide range of applications that run the gamut from data storage to lending unused resources to health care.

4.5.2   dApp Example: The Decentralized Autonomous Organization (DAO)

A DAO is a popular type of dApp whose goal is to codify an organization's rules and decision-making processes, eliminating the need for documents and people in its governing by creating a structure with decentralized control. (See the Uber counter-example in Sect. 4.5.1.)

The DAO provides a particularly useful example because it was programmed by the team behind the German startup Slock.it, a company that builds "smart locks" that let people share their cars, boats, apartments, and other belongings, akin to a decentralized version of Airbnb. The DAO was launched on 30 April, 2016, with a 28-day funding window and raised more than $100 million by 15 May.

However, after the DAO was launched, hackers were successful in stealing a significant portion of its endowment, not because of weaknesses in the Ethereum protocol but because of a programming defect in the DAO smart contract. The community was split as to whether this theft could be reversed, and as a result, the Ethereum blockchain and its currency also split into Ethereum and Ethereum Classic. (We discuss more about cryptocurrency splits in Chap. 5.)

While all networked systems are vulnerable to various kinds of attacks, the Ethereum network has never been hacked and has continuously executed many other smart contracts. Indeed, the Ethereum network was free of bugs and was functioning perfectly when the hack occurred; it was not the Ethereum network but the code of the DAO smart contract that was faulty.

4.6 Turing Completeness

4.6.1 Background

In computability theory, a system of data-manipulation rules (e.g., a computer's instruction set, a programming language, or a cellular automaton) is said to be Turing complete or computationally universal if it can be used to simulate any Turing machine, that is, a mathematical model of a universal computer with only a minimal instruction set.

The concept is named after the English mathematician and computer scientist Alan Turing. The expression power of rule-based grammars was later explained by the Chomsky hierarchy, described by Noam Chomsky in 1956.

A Turing-complete ruleset is theoretically able to express all tasks that a computer can accomplish. Since the programming language used for the Ethereum platform is Turing-complete, any conceivable computer program can be implemented on it.

To show that a ruleset is Turing-complete, it suffices to show that it can be used to simulate some Turing-complete system. For example, an imperative language is Turing-complete if it has conditional branching (e.g., "if" and "goto" statements or a "branch if zero" instruction) and the ability to change an arbitrary amount of memory. In fact, almost all programming languages today are Turing-complete if one sets aside the limitation of finite memory, which is due to physical constraints.

4.6.2 Turing Completeness and Ethereum

Using Solidity and Serpent, one can write applications (smart contracts) that can usually solve any computational problem and can perform looping and branching statements as well as local state storage. This functionality is required to implement most non-trivial computer programs.

Because the EVM is Turing-complete, programs written in other programming languages, such as Java or Python, can also be written in Solidity. Thus, Turing completeness is key to Ethereum smart contracts because it provides the ability to implement any logic.

4.7   Legal Perspective

The digital age is replete with new phenomena: Cryptocurrencies, smart contracts, and the generation of financial resources through pure computing capacities are realities. Digitization requires that legal regulations develop in parallel to protect against unintended law violations by entrepreneurs and to deter bad actors. However, with regard to blockchain, the law remains far from a complete with regard to legality and liability.

Smart contracts occupy a central position in the space of blockchain applications, as they provide direct enforcement of a contract between parties. Thus, they combine traditional contract law and computer science and may, as a result, alter the role of a lawyer or perhaps abolish it altogether. What this assessment overlooks, however, is that legal requirements surrounding the execution of contractual agreements are still governed by traditional law. Even though the discussion regarding smart contract law has yet to unfold fully, it may not have a profound impact on legislation after all.

This debate sparks memories of the "Law of the Horse" debate, a term used in the mid-1990s to define the state of cyberlaw during the early years of the Internet. Judge Frank H. Easterbrook of the United States Court of Appeals for the Seventh Circuit argued against defining cyberlaw as a unique section of legal studies and litigation. Citing Gerhard Casper as having coined the expression "law of the horse," Easterbrook stated that Casper's arguments against specialized or niche legal studies applied to cyberlaw as well as race horses [10]. Therefore, while blockchain-based systems stretch the effectiveness of the existing legal framework because of uncertainty about the law's applicability, as the exact execution location of a smart contract may be unknown, these systems are not likely to require their own set of legal provisions.

4.7.1   Smart Contract Interpretation

One could assume that the code itself represents an offer and an acceptance and that the contract's execution then takes place in the blockchain and not outside it. However, this approach is incompatible with the technical requirements of a smart contract. Nick Szabo, the inventor of the Bitcoin precursor Bit Gold, coined the term "smart contracts" and described these contracts as automated computer programs that can execute contract terms, so the term "smart contract" describes a program that controls and executes legally relevant aspects of a contract but does not constitute the contract itself.

To grasp this subtlety, consider the example of a car leasing contract. In this instance, once the contract has been closed, a code can be used to enforce it (e.g., by locking the car if the payments are not made on time). This situation is comparable to that of the conclusion of a contract at a vending machine, where the offer and acceptance of the contract do not result from the mechanics of the machine but from circumstances outside the machine. The machine's mechanics serve to transfer goods, just as the smart contract controls the leased asset.

4.7.2   Open Questions

A multitude of questions remain: For example, whether smart contracts can be assigned to a legal person (i.e., a human or non-human that is recognized as having certain privileges and obligations) remains to be determined, and legal mechanisms must be put in place to address digital contract malfunctions, such as when the contract unfolds in a way that is disagreeable to the customer or there are differences in the buyer's and seller's evaluations of the result. Any implementation of legal mechanisms will ultimately depend on the locally applicable law, which will not always be trivial to determine given the decentralized nature of the underlying network and unlimited locations of contract code execution.

When a smart contract is concluded, which invariably occurs on a machine, a key question arises regarding to whom the declarations of intent can be attributed. Such considerations arise thanks to the Internet of Things (IoT) (e.g., an empty refrigerator that orders the food itself). There may even be a smart contract running between two machines if, say, the grocery store uses a machine as well.

A simple and uniform solution to these problems does not yet exist. For now, both the responsibility and accountability can be traced back to the chain of attributability, and as with any product, the human being that is ultimately behind setting up an autonomous system. The smart contract constellation discussed in this chapter usually involves two people: the user and the programmer. To whom the transaction is ultimately attributable depends on the degree of the action's autonomy, such that the more autonomous the machine's actions, the sooner the declaration of intent is attributable to the programmer.

Given the distributed nature of most blockchains, an additional concern arises regarding the applicability of the law. The Ethereum network is a distributed global public network, so it is not run on central servers in a certain geographic location; instead, the computing power that runs the network is contributed by nodes that are spread across the globe. Therefore, a user cannot know in advance where his smart contract will be executed—on a node in Germany or one in China—an ambiguity that adds to the legal complexity.

4.7.3   Conclusion

Smart contracts have a large and flexible application framework that will expand with the rapid advances in technology. To remain compliant with the law, this technical progress cannot move outside our current legal framework. However, because of the large scope of smart contracts' applications, legal dilemmas are likely to arise. To cope with the burgeoning minefield of technical and legal complexity and to escape irrelevance, lawyers must move beyond their classic methods and training. Some large research universities (e.g., Oxford and LSE), offer blockchain-specific legal electives, so at least these issues are being touched upon.

4.8   Exercise ("Piggy Bank")

4.8.1   Introduction

This exercise focuses on the deployment of a fully functional smart contact, the "Piggy Bank" contract, which was introduced in Sect. 4.1. By deploying it on your own blockchain, you can explore its working mechanism in full detail. We will try to place money inside the piggy bank, take money out of the piggy bank and validate that all boundary conditions are fulfilled. For example, only the owner of the piggy bank can take money out and only if the pre-set savings threshold (i.e., 1 ETH) has been reached.

To launch the "PiggyBank" smart contract on our private Ethereum blockchain, we must first create three components: the opcode, the bytecode, and the ABI. We will use the Ethereum client "Geth" on our private node to launch the contract and to start the exercise. Prior to performing the exercise, we will briefly introduce these three components and their purpose (Fig. 4.9).

4.8.2   Opcode

Opcode: The opcode specifies the operations that the contract can execute on the Ethereum virtual machine (EVM); these operations are the individual atomic operations, as specified by the Ethereum protocol (Fig. 4.4). The opcode is a pre-compiled version of Solidity code; there is a 1:1 relationship between the smart contract's opcode and bytecode. The opcode is an intermediary step; it is not required per se but can be used as a reference for the interpretability of the contract post compilation.

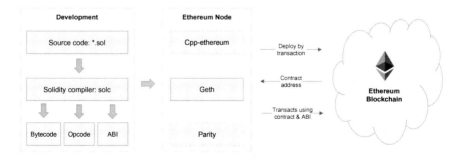

Fig. 4.9 Smart contract deployment (illustrative)

```
PUSH1 0x80 PUSH1 0x40 MSTORE PUSH1 0x4 CALLDATASIZE LT PUSH2 0x1E JUMPI
PUSH1 0x0 CALLDATALOAD PUSH1 0xE0 SHR DUP1 PUSH4 0x45615BCC EQ PUSH2 0x20
JUMPI JUMPDEST STOP JUMPDEST CALLVALUE DUP1 ISZERO PUSH2 0x2C JUMPI PUSH1
0x0 DUP1 REVERT JUMPDEST POP PUSH2 0x35 PUSH2 0x37 JUMP JUMPDEST STOP
JUMPDEST PUSH1 0x0 DUP1 SWAP1 SLOAD SWAP1 PUSH2 0x100 EXP SWAP1 DIV PUSH20
0xFFFFFFFFFFFFFFFFFFFFFFFFFFFFFFFFFFFFFFFF          AND          PUSH20
0xFFFFFFFFFFFFFFFFFFFFFFFFFFFFFFFFFFFFFFFF   AND   CALLER        PUSH20
0xFFFFFFFFFFFFFFFFFFFFFFFFFFFFFFFFFFFFFFFF AND EQ PUSH2 0x90 JUMPI PUSH1
0x0   DUP1   REVERT   JUMPDEST   PUSH8   0xDE0B6B3A7640000  ADDRESS  PUSH20
0xFFFFFFFFFFFFFFFFFFFFFFFFFFFFFFFFFFFFFFFF AND BALANCE LT ISZERO PUSH2 0xBC
JUMPI PUSH1 0x0 DUP1 REVERT JUMPDEST PUSH1 0x0 DUP1 SWAP1 SLOAD SWAP1 PUSH2
0x100 EXP SWAP1 DIV PUSH20 0xFFFFFFFFFFFFFFFFFFFFFFFFFFFFFFFFFFFFFFFF AND
PUSH20  0xFFFFFFFFFFFFFFFFFFFFFFFFFFFFFFFFFFFFFFFF AND PUSH2 0x8FC ADDRESS
PUSH20  0xFFFFFFFFFFFFFFFFFFFFFFFFFFFFFFFFFFFFFFFF AND BALANCE SWAP1 DUP2
ISZERO MUL SWAP1 PUSH1 0x40 MLOAD PUSH1 0x0 PUSH1 0x40 MLOAD DUP1 DUP4 SUB
DUP2 DUP6 DUP9 DUP9 CALL SWAP4 POP POP POP POP ISZERO DUP1 ISZERO PUSH2
0x13A JUMPI RETURNDATASIZE PUSH1 0x0 DUP1 RETURNDATACOPY RETURNDATASIZE
PUSH1 0x0 REVERT JUMPDEST POP JUMP INVALID LOG2 PUSH6 0x627A7A723158
KECCAK256     SWAP1     0xe8     DIFFICULTY     SWAP16     DUP9     PUSH23
0xC53A9A1C0EA79B65F7326CF802B7CC2DC9805C774098B8 DUP8 SWAP16 0x2b PUSH5
0x736F6C6343 STOP SDIV SIGNEXTEND STOP ORIGIN
```

4.8.3 Bytecode

The bytecode is the compiled machine-level code, which is how the smart contract is stored on the on the EVM. The bytecode is a binary representation of the opcodes compiled from the original smart contract source code. The bytecode encodes the commands that are then executed by the individual network nodes.

```
608060405260043610610e5760003560e01c806345615bcc14610020575b005b34801561
002c57600080fd5b5061003561003756b005b6000809054906101000a900473ffffffffff
ffffffffffffffffffffffffffffffff1673ffffffffffffffffffffffffffffffffffffffff
163373ffffffffffffffffffffffffffffffffffffffff161461009057600080fd5b670de0
b6b3a76400003073ffffffffffffffffffffffffffffffffffffffff163110156100bc5760
0080fd5b6000809054906101000a900473ffffffffffffffffffffffffffffffffffffffff
1673ffffffffffffffffffffffffffffffffffffffff166108fc3073ffffffffffffffffffff
ffffffffffffffffffff163190811502906040516000604051808303818588f1935050
505015801561013a573d6000803e3d6000fd5b5056fea265627a7a7231582090e8449f8876
c53a9a1c0ea79b65f7326cf802b7cc2dc9805c774098b8879f2b64736f6c634300050b0032
```

4.8.4 Application Binary Interface (ABI)

The ABI specifies the interface for interacting with the smart contract, including which functions the smart contract comprises, what these functions can be called, and what parameters they can process. The ABI can be interpreted as being like an application programming interface (API).

```
[
    {
        "constant": false,
        "inputs": [],
        "name": "spend",
        "outputs": [],
        "payable": false,
        "stateMutability": "nonpayable",
        "type": "function"
    },
    {
        "inputs": [],
        "payable": false,
        "stateMutability": "nonpayable",
        "type": "constructor"
    },
    {
        "payable": true,
        "stateMutability": "payable",
        "type": "fallback"
    }
]
```

One good way to think about ABI specifications is in terms of the ERK-20 token. All ERK-20 tokens share the same ABI, which make it possible to trade them on the same exchanges and have a common interface for consistency. However, the underlying specifications of each ERK-20 token can be completely different from those of other ERK-20 tokens, and these specifications are defined in its bytecode.

4.8.5   Piggy Bank Deployment

At this point, you already have all the building blocks to deploy the Piggy Bank smart contract (i.e., the contract bytecode and its ABI).

(a) **Reconnect**

First, re-connect to your docker instance. As before, you can always use the console of your operating system to check which docker images are still running by using *docker ps -a* command:

```
>docker ps -a
CONTAINER ID        IMAGE       COMMAND         CREATED       STATUS          PORTS       NAMES
d708bf8dc45d        ubuntu      "/bin/bash"     2 days ago    Exited (255)                pow
```

As before, if your console is no longer running (i.e., as depicted above), you need to re-start the instance by using the *start* command. You can skip this step if your console is still running. Note that your container ID will be different:

```
docker start db253cb81bf7
root@db253cb81bf7:/#
```

Once your node is up and running (or if your node status is *running*), you can re-connect to the console using the *attach* command. Again, note that your container ID will be different:

```
docker attach db253cb81bf7
db253cb81bf7
```

At this point, you should be back at the @root screen; your prompt should look as follows:

```
root@015e2e8bef67:/#
```

As before, we will re-launch the Geth console. The command below launches the Geth console in an interactive mode. Make sure that you are in the test1 folder before you execute this command (i.e., by using the change directory (*cd*) command that we introduced in Chaps. 1 and 2):

```
root@015e2e8bef67:~/test1# geth console --datadir node_pow --mine --miner.threads 1 --nousb
```

(b) **ABI Creation**

Now you will create a new contract specification using the *eth.contract* command, as well as the ABI provided in Sect. 4.8.4:

```
> var bank = eth.contract(
  [
    {
      "constant": false,
      "inputs": [],
      "name": "spend",
      "outputs": [],
      "payable": false,
      "stateMutability": "nonpayable",
      "type": "function"
    },
    {
      "inputs": [],
      "payable": false,
      "stateMutability": "nonpayable",
      "type": "constructor"
    },
    {
      "payable": true,
      "stateMutability": "payable",
      "type": "fallback"
    }
  ]);
```

Next, use the *bank.abi* command to verify that the contract specification has been stored properly:

```
> bank.abi
```

Your output should look as follows:

```
> bank.abi
[{
    constant: false,
    inputs: [],
    name: "spend",
    outputs: [],
    payable: false,
    stateMutability: "nonpayable",
    type: "function"
}, {
    inputs: [],
    payable: false,
    stateMutability: "nonpayable",
    type: "constructor"
}, {
    payable: true,
    stateMutability: "payable",
    type: "fallback"
}]
```

(c) Contract Launch

By storing the ABI specification, you have defined what types of commands your smart contract can accept. However, you have not yet specified what these commands do once the contract is deployed, so you need the bytecode, as provided in Sect. 4.8.3; with the bytecode and the ABI specification, you can now deploy the smart contract on your blockchain.

Just as in the previous exercises, remember to unlock the launch accounts before executing the command below:

```
> personal.unlockAccount(personal.listAccounts[0])
Unlock account 0xe9c51fb5f23321142ee20e991413b956e1c5fbc6
Passphrase:
```

Now you are ready to launch your first smart contract:

```
> var instance = bank.new({data:
"0x6080604052600436100610610016e5760003560e01c806345615bcc14610020575b005b34801561002c57600080fd5b50610035
610037565b005b60008090549061010a900a473ffffffffffffffffffffffffffffffffffffffff1673ffffffffffffffffffff
ffffffffffffffffffffff163373ffffffffffffffffffffffffffffffffffffffff1614610090057600080fd5b670de0b6b3
a76400003073ffffffffffffffffffffffffffffffffffffffff163110156100bc57600080fd5b6000809054906101000a900
473ffffffffffffffffffffffffffffffffffffffff1673ffffffffffffffffffffffffffffffffffffffff166108fc3073ff
ffffffffffffffffffffffffffffffffffffffff163190811502906040516000604051808303818589f1935050505015801566
1013a573d6000803e3d6000fd5b5056fea265627a7a7231582090e8449f8876c53a9a1c0ea79b65f7326cf802b7cc2dc9805c
774098b8879f2b64736f6c634300050b0032", gas: 80000, from: personal.listAccounts[0]});

INFO [09-15|15:41:15.518] Submitted contract creation
fullhash=0x16beef15f4accb456a2779756657773fc07551f048e1a84f42bec0e5a3f034dcd
contract=0xA48582610d3bB3cD524Cf2C76fDed2fB85F17BD0
```

Congratulations! you have just launched your first smart contract! Next, we will interact with this smart contract to ensure that it works as we expect it to. Note that the contract variable is the address of the newly launched contract.

(d) **Interaction**

First, check the balance of your contract just as you checked the balances of your personal accounts, using the contract ID:

```
> eth.getBalance("0xA48582610d3bB3cD524Cf2C76fDed2fB85F17BD0")
0
```

Next, send some money to the smart contract (i.e., put some ETH in the Piggy Bank). Use the same command you used to send money between two accounts. (Use the contract ID from the contact that you just created, not the ID used in the "to" field, as in the example below):

```
web3.eth.sendTransaction (
    {
        from:personal.listAccounts[0],
        to:"0xA48582610d3bB3cD524Cf2C76fDed2fB85F17BD0",
        value:7
    }
);
```

As before, unlock your sender account first. To make life a bit easier, you can use the following command to unlock the account for an extended period of time. You can specify various durations, but setting the duration to 0 will keep the account unlocked until you sign out of the *Geth* console.

```
> personal.unlockAccount(personal.listAccounts[0],"",0)
true
```

Next, let's see if the value of the contract, that is, the money in the piggy bank, was adjusted as we would expect. You can do this using the same method you used to validate the value of your personal accounts after the regular transactions.

```
> eth.getBalance("0xA48582610d3bB3cD524Cf2C76fDed2fB85F17BD0")
0
```

Just as before, first initiate the mining of the contract execution with the same command you used before:

```
> miner.start();
```

You should see in the mining output that your transaction was mined—that is, block 276 contains a new transaction, the money that you sent to the piggy bank:

```
> miner.start()
INFO [09-15|21:41:36.479] Updated mining threads                         threads=2
INFO [09-15|21:41:36.479] Transaction pool price threshold updated  price=1000000000
INFO [09-15|21:41:36.488] Commit new mining work      number=276 sealhash=91_df uncles=0 txs=0 gas=0      fees=0       elapsed=175.3µs
INFO [09-15|21:41:36.488] Commit new mining work      number=276 sealhash=6f_b3 uncles=0 txs=1 gas=21000 fees=2.1e-05 elapsed=671.7µs
INFO [09-15|21:41:39.646] Successfully sealed new block
```

Now you can check the balance of the piggy bank contract using the eth.get-Balance command; you can also validate that (1) no one except personal.listAccounts[0] can withdraw money from this piggy bank, and (2) this withdrawal can only occur once you have sent 1ETH (or more) to the piggy bank.

```
> eth.getBalance("0xA48582610d3bB3cD524Cf2C76fDed2fB85F17BD0")
7
```

References

1. Wood G (nd) Ethereum: a secure decentralised generalised transaction ledger
2. Diedrich H (2016) Ethereum: blockchains, digital assets, smart contracts, decentralized autonomous organizations. Wildfire Publishing, Brookvale
3. Antonopoulos A (2017) Mastering bitcoin: unlocking digital cryptocurrencies. O'Reilly Media, Sebastopol
4. Hodges A (2012) Alan turing: the enigma. Princeton University Press, Princeton
5. Smullyan RM (1992) Gödel's incompleteness theorems. Oxford University Press, New York
6. Wood G, Antonopoulos A (2019) Mastering ethereum: building smart contracts and dApps. O'Reilly, Beijing
7. Flanagan D (2020) JavaScript: the definitive guide. O'Reilly, Sebastopol
8. Dannen C (2017) Introducing ethereum and solidity: foundations of cryptocurrency and blockchain programming for beginners. Apress, New York
9. Bambara J, Allen P (2018) Blockchain: a practical guide to developing business, law, and technology solutions. McGraw-Hill, New York City
10. Barfield W (2015) Cyber-humans: our future with machines. Springer, Cham

Privacy and Anonymity

5

5.1 Introduction

Bitcoin is the world's most transparent payment method in the sense of transaction traceability: Any transaction that occurs on the network can be traced to its origin, and any account that was ever linked to any bitcoin or fraction of a bitcoin is similarly traceable. However, while anyone can see how and when bitcoins have been moved, the identity of the corresponding account's owner is unknown [1]. Therefore, Bitcoin is technically a pseudonymous currency, rather than an anonymous one—a distinction covered in this chapter. As a point of comparison, contrast Bitcoin's transaction traceability to that of real-world financial systems, where opening a bank account requires unambiguous and highly regulated identity verification, but the funds' origin is essentially untraceable by either private or public entities.

It is, perhaps, unsurprising then that the public's perception of Bitcoin has often been shaped by incidents in which Bitcoin has served primarily as the currency of choice for criminal activity because it is an untraceable means of payment for such transactions as financing drug purchases on the infamous Silk Road website [2].

This chapter covers the degrees of anonymity enabled by digital cryptocurrencies, the tools that can be leveraged to that end (e.g., the TOR network), the practices that can be deployed to de-anonymize network nodes (e.g., taint analysis), and the innovative mechanisms used to counteract de-anonymization. We also consider new mechanisms that have recently been put in place to protect the anonymity of major cryptocurrencies (i.e., Bitcoin and Ethereum) transactions, as well as novel concepts like zero-knowledge proofs.

We close this chapter by introducing another set of cryptocurrencies, the so-called privacy coins (e.g., Zerocoin, Zerocash), which are designed to ensure true transaction anonymity. We analyze the mechanisms that were set up to that end and how these mechanisms differ from those deployed in the operations of the pseudonymous Bitcoin network.

© Springer Nature Switzerland AG 2020   99
D. Hellwig et al., *Build Your Own Blockchain*, Management for Professionals,
https://doi.org/10.1007/978-3-030-40142-9_5

5.1.1 Anonymity

Anonymity in the context of cryptocurrencies describes interactions that do not require a name, while pseudonymity describes interactions in which a false name is used. While the terms are often used interchangeably, they differ in a subtle but important way.

A real name is not required for one to interact with the Bitcoin network, but an address (i.e., the public key hash) is, and such an address can serve as an identifier: Although addresses are not directly linked to real identities, the network data can be mined for information about their owners' behavioral patterns, which may or may not reveal their real identities (Sect. 5.2). Therefore, while Bitcoin may appear anonymous since using the currency does not require a real name, the Bitcoin account address itself functions as an identifier, thereby rendering Bitcoin a pseudonymous system.

5.1.2 Unlinkability

To make a pseudonymous system like Bitcoin anonymous, linking addresses and transactions to the same originator should be as difficult as possible, so addresses and transactions must be unlinkable. If addresses and/or transactions can be linked to an originator (i.e., an account/wallet/private key), an external party can analyze the transaction history and an originator's balance. Once an originator's identity is exposed (e.g., using side channels), the originator's transaction history and wealth are also exposed. Thus the property of unlinkability reflects primarily on the capabilities of an external third party: If the owner of a cryptocurrency address (e.g., Bitcoin) interacts with the system repeatedly, unlinkability ensures that no external third party can connect the interactions.

A Bitcoin user who is concerned about her anonymity wants to ensure that it is not feasible to link a payment's sender and ultimate recipient by examining the blockchain. As a result, a variety of methods and new, specialized cryptocurrencies with built-in anonymity protocols have emerged. We examine these methods and currencies in more detail in Sects. 5.4, 5.5, and 5.8.

5.1.3 Anonymity Versus Pseudonymity

Online forums are good real-world examples of the difference between anonymity and pseudonymity (Fig. 5.1). In online forums like Quora, users create an account and choose a long-term pseudonym; then they can post under that pseudonym or set up multiple accounts and use multiple pseudonyms. With Quora's pseudonymous model, users can also build their reputations over time. For example, if user dpa_dataGeek88 answers a certain type of question repeatedly, she may become known as a subject-matter expert in this area.

Fig. 5.1 Degrees of anonymity

It is also possible to infer information about a user by collecting her metadata (e.g., time patterns of activity, style of language used). To protect her privacy, a user can set up multiple online identities, one for each contribution; similarly, Bitcoin users can create a new address for each transaction they conduct. However, while theoretically possible, such an approach is impractical, so interactions on Quora (and Bitcoin) are pseudonymous but not anonymous. Still, systems like 4Chan allow users to post messages on a bulletin board anonymously, without individual attribution: Every post is separate and cannot be linked to other posts by the same or any other user.

The interactions that occur on the Bitcoin network are pseudonymous. Chapter 2 showed that the Bitcoin blockchain is permissionless (public), so any individual can retrieve any Bitcoin transaction that has taken place. As such, it is possible to filter for transactions that originated from a specific address. If a Bitcoin address is once associated with the owner's real identity, then all related transactions past and future can also be linked to the same identity.

What's more, even if a direct link between a transaction (or a post) and an individual can be avoided, the pseudonymous profile can be de-anonymized, albeit partially, using so-called side channels. For example, an attacker may examine data that is attributable to pseudonymous Bitcoin transactions, that is, the transaction data stored publicly on the blockchain, and make certain inferences by, for example, zeroing in on a user's likely geographic location by analyzing the times when a given user was active. The attacker can then integrate this data with other information sources.

When analyzing the activity of a pseudonymous identity (often referred to as "handle"), an attacker may review the usage data from multiple semi-public accounts (e.g., Twitter, Quora). Correlating this data can provide additional insights about a user's behavioral patterns, such as activity times over certain periods, and, thus, indicators of her location based on time zones. For instance, Satoshi Nakamoto frequently published changes to the Bitcoin code repository from UTC 13:00 to UTC 06:00, which suggested that he resided somewhere in the Americas (if he worked during the day). Metadata may also unintentionally reveal identifying information: John McAfee's "hiding" location was once accidentally revealed in the geo-tagging metadata included in one of the images posted by journalists on Twitter.

Therefore, it is possible to create loose links between a real-world identity (or at least a pseudonymous identity, such as an online account) and the user's Bitcoin address. While the process of de-anonymizing users might seem complicated, laborious, and time-consuming, it is surprisingly easy to execute. Thus, pseudonymity without unlinkability guarantees neither privacy nor anonymity.

5.1.4 Taint Analysis

Using publicly available Bitcoin transaction data, external parties can run various types of analyses to gain insights into the owner of a Bitcoin address. Taint analysis, just one measure of the (lack of) anonymity that Bitcoin provides, is a particularly popular method of calculating the degree to which two addresses are related, that is, the extent to which one address is "tainted" by another. For instance, during the investigation of Silk Road, a darknet marketplace for illegal goods and services, the FBI used taint analysis to track bitcoins from Silk Road to a wallet found on the perpetrator's private laptop: If bitcoins sent by an address S always end up at some other address R, whether directly or after passing through intermediate addresses, then S and R will have a high taint score.

More specifically, the taint analysis calculates the correlation between two addresses as the percentage of bitcoins that originate from the same address in an individual transaction. In the example in Fig. 5.2, A_1 has a taint of 50 percent with respect to A_4, while A_3 has a taint of 75 percent, and A_2 has a taint of 25 percent [3]. In determining a taint score, the formula also accounts for transactions with multiple inputs and/or outputs.

This cursory example reveals only direct connections in the transaction graph and does not consider contextual information (e.g., side-channel information). Malicious third-party actors who are looking for information may use additional data, such as the timing of transactions and relative transaction size, to de-anonymize transactions. An even more intricate approach relies on the use of idiosyncrasies in wallet software (e.g., CVE-2013-2272, which allow third parties to link a public IP address with a public key). More on that later in this chapter.

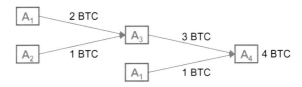

Fig. 5.2 Taint analysis

5.2 De-anonymization

5.2.1 Introduction

This chapter introduces the common techniques used to de-anonymize the Bitcoin network and the enhanced anonymization methods that have been developed in response. As we shall see, Bitcoin is neither fully anonymous nor fully traceable.

5.2.2 Transaction Graph Analysis

Suppose that the donation page of an NGO group has a "refresh" button next to the Bitcoin address for donations. The refresh button allows the NGO group to generate a new Bitcoin address for each donation it receives, a common best practice, so every donor sends its donation to a separate address, all of which are controlled by the NGO group. Thus, it might appear that these different addresses are unlinkable.

However, suppose now that the NGO group wants to purchase a new computer that costs ten bitcoins (10 BTC). Let's assume that there are three separate donations, each with their respective funds (e.g., 2BTC, 3BTC, and 5 BTC) that are captured as unspent transaction outputs. Since the NGO group does not have a single address with 10 bitcoins, it must combine three of the donation outputs to use as inputs for the computer purchase transaction. This output combination is recorded permanently in the blockchain, as are the three donation inputs. An attacker who analyzes this public data could then conclude that the three transactions used for the computer purchase are controlled by a single owner, and as more bitcoins are spent in this fashion, more details about the relationships between the individual donation addresses and the receiver can be uncovered, thus moving toward de-anonymizing both.

5.2.3 Network-Layer De-anonymization

In addition to de-anonymizing transactions by grouping individual Bitcoin addresses, it is possible to take advantage of the network structure to reveal the identity of users.

Network-layer de-anonymization leverages the workings of the Bitcoin network. To transact on the blockchain, a user must broadcast a message to the Bitcoin network, which is then distributed to all the other network nodes. In broadcasting information to the rest of the network, a network node will attempt to communicate with the largest number of other nodes possible, reaching the nodes geographically closest to it first.

If an actor controls enough nodes in various locations, that actor can determine the location of the first node that broadcasts a transaction, that is, the node that is run by the transaction originator. The actor does this by measuring and comparing the time it takes to receive the information at the various locations of his different nodes (i.e., triangulation).

Network-layer de-anonymization poses several problems, not least of which is its utility to authoritative regimes, so additional anonymization methods are needed.

5.3 The Onion Router (TOR) Network

5.3.1 Background

One common approach to ensuring a user's anonymity in any network is the so-called TOR browser. Online surveillance methods (e.g., tracking IP addresses) can directly compromise individual users' privacy, as encryption alone does not ensure anonymity. The packet headers, which are small pieces of data about the data, that are part of any internet-based communication activities can reveal significant information about a user's online activity, such as the services and websites she is using to communicate. Therefore, robust anonymity can be guaranteed only with a system that can provide full end-to-end anonymity. Enter TOR: "The Onion Routing project."

The TOR network (or TOR) allows users to access the internet anonymously [4]. While the open-source TOR project idea was originally conceived to protect U.S. intelligence communications, it has since found many other uses, including for privacy-conscious individuals who are weary of companies' collecting their usage data, and journalists and activists who are concerned about the consequences of speaking about tyrannical regimes. TOR has also been used for criminal and illicit activities (e.g., sale of counterfeit currency, drugs). While illicit commercial activities via the TOR browser existed long before the emergence of Bitcoin and other cryptocurrencies, they have since flourished precisely because cryptocurrencies enable trusted transactions that hide the identities of the parties involved.

Given the guaranteed anonymity of data transfer when one uses TOR, differentiating non-malicious from malicious usage is difficult. The very purpose of TOR, its ability to make communication anonymous, also makes it essentially impossible to assess the nature of its uses at a technical level. As of the writing of this book, most jurisdictions agree that communication privacy and security are both fundamental rights, but some governments still block access to the TOR software and network–most notably the United Kingdom and, perhaps less surprisingly, Iran and the People's Republic of China [5].

5.3.2 TOR Approach

TOR is a distributed, anonymous communication service that relies on an overlay network that allows individuals to access the Internet anonymously (Fig. 5.3). Users who access websites using the TOR network cannot be tracked, and they can

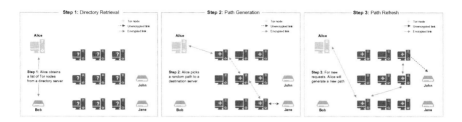

Fig. 5.3 TOR network operations

circumvent any attempts by local Internet providers to block certain content. The TOR network also enables users to share content without revealing the site's hosting location.

TOR's key components are:

- An overlay Network (ON) that selects and connects a subset of nodes in the network.
- Onion Routers (OR) that route traffic.
- An Onion Proxy (OP) that fetches directories and creates virtual network circuits.

TOR runs on top of TCP/IP (Transmission Control Protocol/Internet Protocol), the basic communication language (protocol) of the internet. The TOR network also relies on Transport Layer Security (TLS), the successor to the Secure Sockets Layer (SSL). TLS is a hybrid encryption protocol for secure communication on the Internet. A separate TLS layer is redundant for TOR websites since the TOR system already provides end-to-end encryption. However, when one browses websites via TOR, TLS becomes increasingly important, as the exit node can eavesdrop on one's traffic in clear text and even manipulate it.

As another precautionary measure, data is sent in fixed-size packets or cells, each of which is 514 bytes long—or 512 bytes in the past, which is still reflected in some documentation—so any data transmitted through TOR occurs in multiples of 514 bytes. If the data sent is smaller than one cell, the cell is padded with zeros. This approach makes it harder for intermediaries to guess exactly how many bytes one is communicating with at each step [6].

5.3.3 TOR Usage

To use TOR, the user must first download a TOR client software, such as the TOR Browser. The TOR client then connects to the TOR network and provides a list of all available peers who can route the traffic for the user (i.e., other users who are already part of the system); these other users are the TOR nodes. All nodes must provide public keys to authenticate themselves in the TOR network.

Table 5.1 TOR communication matrix

	User	First relay (entry node)	Second relay (middle node)	Third relay (exit node)	Website
User	✓	✓			
First relay	✓	✓	✓		
Second relay	✓	✓	✓		
Third relay	✓		✓	✓	✓
Website	✓			✓	✓

Once the new user receives the list of TOR network relay nodes, a route through the TOR network is randomly chosen for a set period. A request is usually routed via at least three relay nodes to provide full anonymization.

Anonymity is established because only the user has all the information necessary to reconstruct the full communication path. Public-private key encryption ensures that each relay node sees only its part of the communication. None of the relay nodes, the visited website, or even other Internet services used have enough information to know fully who is communicating with whom (Table 5.1). As of 2019, the network has more than 6,500 nodes.

Furthermore, TOR does not maintain the same route forever, as after about ten minutes, a new random route is chosen, which increases the degree of anonymization and makes tracking traffic virtually impossible. Therefore, any communication between the individual servers is always fully encrypted.

5.3.4 Limitations

TOR-based solutions for providing end-to-end anonymity for communicating with a blockchain network are not always practical, given the overhead and technical expertise required. Other less cumbersome mechanisms have been put in place to address the problem of anonymity of transactions on the blockchain, one of which is called mixing.

5.4 Mixing Models

The most intuitive approach to combating transaction graph analysis is called mixing, which delivers anonymity through an intermediary. Mixing group transactions together makes their origins harder to trace [7].

In the realm of mixing models, the most common strategy requires using multiple mixes in a serial fashion, rather than relying on a single mix (Fig. 5.4). Using multiple mixes reduces a transacting user's reliance on the correctness, integrity, and effectiveness of a single mix in the sequence because it is unlikely that an attacker has compromised all the mixes in use at a given point in time. In addition,

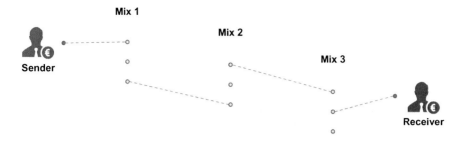

Fig. 5.4 Illustration of a mixing model

the anonymization process will remain unbroken even if a mix is compromised (e.g., the input and output data are shared), as an attacker needs the inputs and outputs from all the other mixes. Therefore, as long as a single mix in the group remains honest and deletes its transaction records, no one will be able to connect the inputs and outputs of the overall process later on, even if a bad actor obtains the information from all of the other mixes in the sequence.

Notably, the well-established approach of employing multiple mixes relies on operating principles that are like those of the TOR network (i.e., multiple transaction layers).

5.5   Decentralized Mixing

5.5.1   Motivation

The benefits of the mixing strategy for anonymization are undeniable, but its implementation has its challenges: To execute a mixed transaction, users must first identify each other, and given that control of the transactions must be pooled, it is unclear that thefts can be avoided. Furthermore, by organizing mixed transactions centrally, one party will still have to obtain all the relevant information (i.e., source addresses, amounts), which is a form of centralized organization that is antithetic to the philosophy of Bitcoin and other decentralized cryptocurrencies.

As a result, various decentralized mixing models have been proposed for both the Bitcoin and the Ethereum ecosystems. Here we focus on one model, Coinjoin, for illustration, but the same approach can be applied to other coins.

5.5.2   Coinjoin Model

The Coinjoin decentralized mixing approach was proposed by core Bitcoin developer Greg Maxwell in 2013. The model describes a group of Bitcoin users who come together to create a single Bitcoin transaction consisting of input transactions of equal value from each user (Fig. 5.5). The users' private keys do not have to be centrally collected for this transaction to occur, as every input signature involved is different from every other. In addition, each user must provide an output address, which will then be mixed to curtail traceability to the originating account. To achieve even greater anonymity, multiple mixing rounds are employed. Thus, anyone who attempts a taint analysis on Bitcoin addresses to identify transaction patterns will not be able to follow the trail. While such an analysis can still find the direct mapping between the input and output transactions, it must assume that the transaction pairings are random, as senders and recipients are mixed.

Therefore, the high-level steps that comprise any Coinjoin transaction are to:

1. Identify several other users to partake in the Coinjoin transactions.
2. Exchange input and output addresses with the other users.
3. Construct a single central aggregated transaction.
4. Distribute the aggregated transaction to all involved users. (All must sign)
5. Post the transaction publicly. (After all signatures are provided).

With this approach, all users can confirm that their target addresses are part of the aggregated transaction prior to providing their signatures. The transaction can be executed only if all users sign the transaction; if a single user refuses to provide his signature, the transaction cannot be posted.

5.5.3 Coinjoin Anonymity

To obtain a specific input-output mapping on a de-centralized mixing model, an attacker can infiltrate a Coinjoin transaction by creating many identities, thus obtaining all but one of the input-output mappings; if successful, that one mapping can be identified.

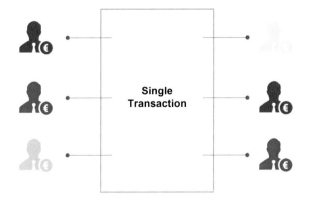

Fig. 5.5 Decentralized mixing via a single pooled transaction

With decentralized mixing models, the users do not know who their peers are, and for the model to work, all input and output addresses must be communicated to all peers involved. Therefore, the question is whether there is an alternative approach to de-anonymizing the transaction that does not require such linking of inputs and outputs.

Posed as such, this problem is no longer a Bitcoin anonymity problem but a general communications anonymity problem. Earlier in this chapter (in Sect. 5.3), we introduced the TOR browser, which allows individuals to interact with the internet without revealing their identities. A similar approach can be employed here to ensure users' anonymity.

Conceptually, the solution consists of three steps:

1. Peers connect and exchange input addresses.
2. Peers disconnect and shuffle their identities.
3. Peers re-connect and exchange output addresses.

In practice, this process can be implemented using an anonymous routing protocol (e.g., decryption mixnets).

5.6 Zero-Knowledge Proofs

5.6.1 Introduction

Zero Knowledge Proofs are mechanisms through which Person A can prove to Person B that Person A knows a secret without revealing any details about the secret to Person B [8]. Such proofs must meet the following criteria:

- Completeness: If the prover's statement is true, it will convince a verifier.
- Soundness: If the prover's statement is false, it cannot convince the verifier.
- Zero-knowledge: If the statement is true, the verifier does not learn any information other than that the prover's statement is true.

In the realm of cryptocurrencies, there is great interest in zero-knowledge proofs, especially as they relate to ensuring anonymity. One way to think about zero-knowledge proofs is via passwords and hashing: When we log in, we do so by typing in a password that only we know. The website uses a hash function to calculate a hash value from our input; that is, the password is converted into a unique sequence of numbers. The website then compares the hash value of the input to the stored hash value, and if they match, the site knows that we have entered the correct password. Thus, the server does not know the actual password ("zero knowledge") but can verify whether a password is correct or not ("proof").

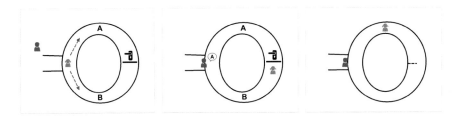

Fig. 5.6 The strange cave of Alibaba

Example: The Strange Cave of Alibaba

The "Strange Cave of Alibaba" provides a helpful illustration of the mechanism of a zero-knowledge proof. The setup involves a cave with one entrance and a locked door with a numeric key that is inside the cave (Fig. 5.6).

In this scenario, prover A wants to show person B, whom prover A knows, the key to unlock the door without revealing what the code is. Prover A enters the cave and calls out to person B, asking from which side of the cave he should exit. To accomplish this task multiple times in a row, prover A must know the code to the door to return from either side of the circular tunnel; in Fig. 5.6, person B asks prover A to exit from the A side.

5.7 Privacy and Security Protocols

5.7.1 Introduction

Data security and privacy are two of the most contentious and critical aspects of security tokens: Both issues pose significant technical challenges, and lapses in ensuring either can jeopardize the foundation of crypto securities.

To explain the nature of these challenges in the realm of security tokens, we draw a comparison to traditional securitized products: Financial securities operate within trusted boundaries that are established among a relatively small number of centralized authorities, and regulations ensure the privacy and protection of transactions that involve financial securities. In contrast, the premise of crypto securities is to disintermediate many of those trusted boundaries using computation logic while remaining compliant with privacy regulations. To that end, many of the existing privacy and protection regulations are transformed into decentralized, blockchain-based protocols.

To illustrate the privacy challenges that arise in the context of security tokens, consider two common scenarios:

1. A tokenized asset issued in Germany is subject to data-protection regulation that stipulates that it can be traded only between German parties and that data related to the trade cannot leave German jurisdiction.
2. An asset-based tokenized product must comply with FINRA rules that ensure the protection of sensitive information related to asset trades.

The first scenario presents the friction between privacy and decentralization, and the second highlights the conflict between privacy and compliance. Both scenarios are examples of the security-token trilemma, which states that security-token architectures are designed to optimize only two of three capabilities: privacy, decentralization, and compliance.

Regulatory bodies do not provide the necessary tools—digital certificates for individual and corporate entities, data brokerages for know-your-customer (KYC), anti-money-laundering (AML), and other "oracle" services—to allow for technologically advanced implementation of their rules. In practice, this regulatory limitation indicates that there is a case for relying on protocols like ZK-SNARKS for security but also that such a technology-based implementation will not necessarily be compliant with certain regulations [9]. Similarly, security-token networks that focus on privacy and compliance are likely to sacrifice decentralization to some degree. This privacy dilemma is one of those dynamics that will influence the next generation of security-token protocols. We examine some of the early implementations of privacy coins next.

5.8 Privacy Coins

5.8.1 Introduction

Unlike the cryptocurrencies that we have seen so far (e.g., Bitcoin, Ethereum), privacy coins are based on cryptocurrency protocols that follow a privacy-first approach. These protocols were designed to address a critical weakness in the existing cryptocurrency space, that is, the lack of real privacy guarantees akin to those that emerge from using cash.

The first chapters of this book explained that the Bitcoin network provides a decentralized mechanism for exchanging crypto tokens (i.e., origination and transfer). However, Bitcoin's greatest strength is also its greatest limitation. Because of the permissionless nature of the decentralized ledger, it is possible to view the history of any payment that has ever occurred, thereby allowing an external party to access transaction information and to identify patterns in the transaction's data. The Bitcoin protocol and its software application addresses this limitation in two ways:

1. Bitcoin transactions occur between public keys (as identifiers) only; public keys are not linked to the names of their owners.
2. The Bitcoin client software can generate an unlimited number of public keys (i.e., identities), thereby protecting users from being tracked.

However, research has shown that these protection mechanisms are insufficient to guarantee true anonymity for Bitcoin users, as in some cases users' identities, although not their real names, can be revealed. Meta information and advanced analyses may enable any party to connect transactions, identify interrelated payments, and trace the activities of individual Bitcoin users over time.

This limitation manifests a major weakness of the Bitcoin protocol. A common solution is the use of Bitcoin "laundries," which employ mixing models to obfuscate a user's transaction history by mixing their transactions with those of other users (see Sect. 5.4). However, Bitcoin laundries also suffer from a variety of drawbacks. For example, the laundries themselves can be compromised, and a critical mass of transactions must be pooled together to obscure an individual transaction's origins if they are to operate effectively.

As we have seen, it is also possible to combine several solutions (e.g., TOR and mixing networks) to achieve both anonymity and obscurity regarding the nature of a transaction. However, these approaches are not yet comprehensive or integrated, leaving room for user error and ambiguity. As a result, alternative solutions like the Zero currencies have emerged that obscure user transactions more holistically by hiding their origin, destination, and amount.

5.8.2 The Zero Currencies

The Zerocoin and Zerocash protocols extend the functionality of the original Bitcoin protocol (Fig. 5.7). Their currencies were the first cryptocurrencies to use zero-knowledge proofs to enable true transactional anonymity.

Zerocoin is a cryptocurrency that obscures the transacting parties' identities by using a mixing model that is built directly into the Zerocoin protocol so there is no need to trust the mixes or peers to ensure anonymity. Zerocash operates in a similar fashion but also obscures the transaction amounts.

Using either Zerocoin or Zerocash comes with tradeoffs. Zerocash is less prone to privacy timing attacks than Zerocoin is, given the significant restriction of transaction data available to the broader network. However, this additional level of privacy can lead to potentially undetected hyper-inflation in Zerocash's money supply, as the fraudulent creation of new money could go unnoticed since transactions cannot be tracked.

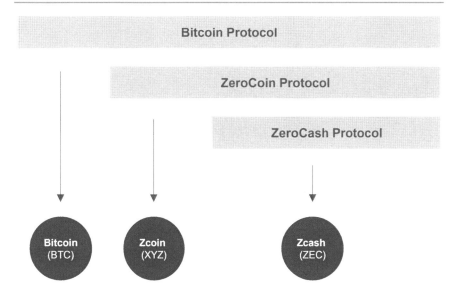

Fig. 5.7 Protocol inheritance

5.8.3 Zerocoin

Zerocoin was initially designed to be part of the existing cryptographic currency bitcoin and to provide more anonymity to users and transactions than bitcoin does. Eventually, Zerocoin became a separate system and was realized as another altcoin (Chap. 2).

The Zerocoin extension would have acted like a money-laundering pool for bitcoin transactions, temporarily pooling bitcoins together in exchange for a temporary currency called Zerocoins. While the laundering pool is an established concept that is already used by several currency-laundering services (Sects. 5.4 and 5.5), Zerocoin implemented this functionality at the protocol level, thereby eliminating any reliance on trusted third parties (i.e., laundries). The protocol anonymizes the exchanges to and from the pool using cryptographic principles, and as a proposed extension to the Bitcoin protocol, it would record the transactions within the existing Bitcoin blockchain.

However, instead of becoming an extension of Bitcoin, Zerocoin was implemented in late 2016 as a fully separate cryptocurrency (XZC). Creating Zerocoins requires selecting a number of coins that a user wants to mint and paying a fee of 0.01 XZC, which increases the level of anonymity by differing the amount paid from the amount spent. For example, if you mint 1653 XZC and then spend exactly 1653 XZC later, it would be easier to trace the transaction back to you than it would be if the two amounts differed.

A user must wait about seventy minutes before transferring newly minted Zerocoins. Once the user sends a transaction, a pre-specified receiver's address obtains the Zerocoins with no transaction history.

Zerocoins always rely on a secondary currency called a basecoin. Basecoins can be converted into Zerocoins and back to break the link between the basecoin (i.e., its transaction history) and the original owner.

An individual Zerocoin can be considered a "proof" token that shows that its owner (1) owned a basecoin at some point and (2) made this basecoin unspendable (which the Zerocoin miners can validate). This proof of a Zerocoin then gives the owner the right to redeem a new basecoin at any later time as a separate coin with no transaction history linked to it.

Zerocoins exist only in standard denominations (e.g., 1, 5, 10). Anyone can generate new Zerocoins off-chain, but these Zerocoins obtain their value only once they are added to the blockchain, after the miners validate them.

The use of Zerocoins is not without its challenges, as the user must consider how to construct the proof that he or she owned a basecoin and made it unspendable and how to validate the proof's uniqueness (i.e., how to avoid double-spending).

Minting a Zerocoin

Before delving into the Zerocoin-minting process, let us first revisit the concept of zero-knowledge proofs, which we introduced in Sect. 5.6. There are three key steps to creating a new Zerocoin, a process that is similar to the hashing mechanisms (Sect. 5.8.3):

- Generate a random serial number S, which will eventually become public.
- Generate a random secret r that will not become public to ensure unlinkability.
- Compute a function H(S, r).

The Zerocoin is then minted only when the miners add it to the blockchain (Fig. 5.8). The pre-generated Zerocoin and basecoin are required as inputs for this mint transaction. The coin is added to the Zerocoin blockchain only if the miners validate the previous destruction of a basecoin.

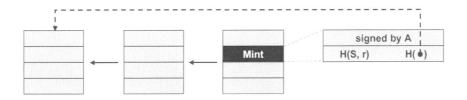

Fig. 5.8 Mint transaction illustration

Spending a Zerocoin

To spend a Zerocoin, the owner reveals the previously generated S, and the other network nodes (miners) subsequently verify that S has not been spent before. Using a zero-knowledge proof, the owner then shows that knows a number r, such that H(S, r) is one of the Zerocoins on the blockchain

Once these claims have been verified, the owner can claim any of the Zerocoins that anyone has added to the blockchain and use them as inputs for a new transaction (i.e., spend them). The newly selected Zerocoins will be devoid of transaction history because r is a secret input, so no one can determine which Zerocoin originally belonged to the user's serial number S. Thus, anonymity is fully realized.

5.8.4   Zerocash

The Zerocash project provides a privacy-preserving version of Bitcoin (i.e., untraceable e-cash). This privacy coin, developed subsequent to Zerocoin, improves on Zerocoin in that transaction amounts in the Zerocash currency are not public, and both the receiver and the sender can remain anonymous [10]. Transaction amounts are visible only to the sender and the receiver, as the decentralized ledger traces only the existence of the transactions. In addition, while units of the Zerocoin currency can be minted only in fixed denominations (e.g., 1, 25, 50, 100), Zerocash removes these limitations and allows for the creation of arbitrary amounts.

From a technical perspective, a key limitation of Zerocash is that a set of secret input parameters is required to set up the system. These inputs must then be securely destroyed, as anyone with access to the inputs can compromise the system.

Functionality

Like Zerocoin, Zerocash creates a separate anonymous currency that exists alongside a (non-anonymous) base currency, which we refer to as basecoin. Users can convert (non-anonymous) basecoins into (anonymous) Zerocoins.

Like Zerocoin, Zerocash's functionality is realized using just two types of transactions, mint transactions and pour transactions, and like Bitcoin transactions, Zerocash transactions are broadcast and appended to a decentralized ledger. The processes for both types of transactions are outlined below.

Mint transactions   A mint transaction allows a user to convert a specified number of non-anonymous bitcoins from an existing Bitcoin address into the same number of Zerocash coins that belong to a specific Zerocash address. The mint transaction itself consists of a cryptographic commitment to a new coin that specifies the coin's value, the owner's address, and a unique serial number. The commitment is based on the SHA-256 hash function and hides both the coin's value and the owner's address.

Individual Zerocash nodes maintain a Merkle tree over all of the coin commitments seen thus far, so any user can demonstrate ownership of a coin commitment via its decommitted values, as well as through a short witness of membership in the tree. Publishing this information as an "ownership proof" is not private, so a second type of transaction, the pour transaction, is required to ensure privacy. The pour transaction, allows a user to prove that he has knowledge of such information without having to share it.

Pour transactions A pour transaction allows a user to make a private payment by consuming some number of the coins he owns to produce new coins. In general, a pour transaction for (up to) two input coins and (up to) two output coins, involves proving, without sharing the keys that control the coins (i.e., according to a zero-knowledge mechanism), that:

1. The user owns the two input coins.
2. Each one of the input coins appears in some previous mint transaction or as the output coin of some previous pour transaction.
3. The value of the input coins equals the value of the output coins.

The pour transaction consumes the input coins by revealing their serial numbers but does not reveal any other information, such as the input or output coins' value or their owners' addresses. The pour transaction can also output some (non-anonymous) bitcoins to transfer Zerocoins back into (non-anonymous) bitcoins or to pay transaction fees.

The commitment contained in a mint transaction is constructed so anyone can verify that the committed coin has the value claimed. For a pour transaction, anyone can verify that the zero-knowledge proof contained therein is valid (and that a few other invariants hold).

However, for efficiency, Zerocash does not use just any zero-knowledge proof but leverages zero-knowledge Succinct Non-interactive ARguments of Knowledge (zk-SNARK) systems, which are zero-knowledge proofs that are particularly short and easy to verify. Such proofs require less than 300 bytes of storage space and can be verified in only a few milliseconds.

5.9 Exercise

5.9.1 Introduction

In this exercise, we review a few of the privacy-related elements of the blockchain ecosystem and take a closer look at the individual blocks and the data that they contain. We described the blockchain-enabled cryptocurrency system as more transparent in the sense that all transactions can be traced. As part of this exercise, we show how the data required for such efforts can be accessed in practice.

As before, we will be working with the Ethereum-based blockchain environment. While the specific commands are different, the same principles are applicable to the Bitcoin blockchain.

First, follow the steps outlined in Chap. 1 to set up an Ethereum-based blockchain on your virtual docker instance using the Geth distribution, and initialize the (local) mining process. You should pre-fund the initial account and then create a second account so we can conduct a sample transaction between these two accounts. You can follow the steps below to create this set-up:

1. **Environment Prep**

Before you can create the sample transaction that we will analyze in this chapter, you need to create one additional account. This account will not be pre-funded, which will make it easier for you to validate that a transaction did take place. From in the Geth console, use the following command to create a new account, just as you did in Chap. 2. Type in a passphrase that will not be visible on the screen:

```
> personal.newAccount()
Passphrase:
Repeat passphrase:
"0xa53f495b27a40b73e0919b89aa8e15d5c220199b"
```

You can validate that you have currently (at least) two active accounts by using the `personal.listAccounts` command in the Geth console:

```
> personal.listAccounts
[
    "0xe9c51fb5f23321142ee20e991413b956e1c5fbc6",
    "0xa53f495b27a40b73e0919b89aa8e15d5c220199b"
]
```

2. **Block Determination**

The starting point for this exercise should be the state you reach after creating the DAG file. As before, your local client node will automatically start the mining work, and you should see the following output periodically for each block.

```
INFO [09-14|16:56:03.375] Successfully sealed new block      number=49 sealhash=d0e…51a hash=ede…b9b elapsed=9.347s
INFO [09-14|16:56:03.375] ⊶ block reached canonical chain    number=42 hash=b02…413
INFO [09-14|16:56:03.375] ⚲ mined potential block            number=49 hash=ede…b9b
INFO [09-14|16:56:03.375] Commit new mining work             number=50 sealhash=18e…981 uncles=0 txs=0 gas=0 fees=0 elapsed=261.3µs
```

The first part of this exercise is to conduct another sample transaction between two accounts, as you did in Chap. 2. Repeat these steps (i.e., set up two new accounts (A, B) and execute a sample transaction of 100 wei from account A to B).

If your blockchain is running and you have your two accounts created (as well as one of them funded), you can execute the transfer using the web3.eth. sendTransaction command with the two accounts as follows. (Don't forget to unlock the account first):

```
web3.eth.sendTransaction
(
    {
        from:personal.listAccounts[0],
        to:personal.listAccounts[1],
        value:1000
    }
);
"0x45b85025de231fd7641d475f0144bc130433cd843ea0190ac985b4734f889aa8"
```

Next, determine in which block this transaction was included. To that end, first figure out which block is currently being mined by your local blockchain instance using the *eth.getBlock* command:

```
> web3.eth.blockNumber
7
```

From the output, you can determine that the client is currently mining block number 7. Note that you are working with low block numbers because you are always starting a new blockchain instances for your exercises. As a point of reference, as of the writing of this book in late 2019, the current block of the Ethereum blockchain is 8,662,404, and the current block of the Bitcoin blockchain is 597,531. Even though the Bitcoin blockchain started much earlier, there are more Ethereum blocks because of the shorter mining time: Ethereum blocks are mined every 10–20 seconds, while Bitcoin blocks are mined only every 10 minutes.

3. **Block Analysis**

Using the web3.eth.getBlock command and by indicating a block number, you can look at the details of the of any individual block. We provide a sample of the resulting output below. You should be able to replicate this on your private blockchain instance. Following the output, we provide a brief summary of each attribute (Table 5.2).

```
> web3.eth.getBlock(8)
  {
    difficulty: 461939,
    extraData: "0xd8830108158467657468886676f312e31312e34856c696e7578",
    gasLimit: 5802763,
    gasUsed: 0,
    hash: "0x66c678fa0e1da6ca0c36999dc3ea4cb2e4b3707a6c5e21d386de52f706bc5b22",
    logsBloom: "0x00000....0000000",
    miner: "0xe9c51fb5f23321142ee20e991413b956e1c5fbc6",
    mixHash: "0x50c5025174d13a67ac9d8b4991100e874e6af3faa27c429be6520c70b03f4db5",
    nonce: "0x64fc6658c65743b3",
    number: 8,
    parentHash: "0x8c148d837d089b2693c6f0cea1aed859f20fedf9ee23bc03b8655cb11d3b19cc",
    receiptsRoot: "0x56e81f171bcc55a6ff8345e692c0f86e5b48e01b996cadc001622fb5e363b421",
    sha3Uncles: "0x1dcc4de8dec75d7aab85b567b6ccd41ad312451b948a7413f0a142fd40d49347",
    size: 537,
    stateRoot: "0x20ad5c01068e5f39b4dc912adce540c37e38f09bf693316c913ff22b26b48fe7",
    timestamp: 1568542461,
    totalDifficulty: 109318729,
    transactions: [],
    transactionsRoot: "0x56e81f171bcc55a6ff8345e692c0f86e5b48e01b996cadc001622fb5e363b421",
    uncles: []
  }
```

Because block number 8 is the latest block, we can conclude that the sample transaction must have been included in one of the previous seven blocks. In addition, from the data on block 8 displayed before, you can see that it did not

Table 5.2 Block data attributes

Attribute	Data type	Description
difficulty	String	A value indicating the difficulty level applied during the nonce discovering of this block
extraData	String	An optional field (max. 32 bytes) to conserve data for eternity on the Blockchain
gasLimit	Number	A value equal to the current chain-wide limit of gas expenditure per block
gasUsed	Number	The total amount of gas used by all transactions in this block
Hash	String	Hash of the block
logsBloom	String	The bloom filter for the logs of the block; this field facilitates scanning for block data
Miner	String	The address of the beneficiary to whom the mining rewards were given
mixHash	String	A hash that, when combined with the nonce, proves that a sufficient amount of computation was expended
nonce	String	Result of the mining process iteration that satisfies the mining target
number	Number	The block number in the sequence of all block of the blockchain
parentHash	String	The hash of the entire parent block's header (including its nonce and mixhash)
receiptsRoot	String	The root of the receipts trie of the block (i.e., outcomes)
sha3Uncles	String	SHA3 of the uncles data in the block
Size	Number	Integer indicating the size of this block in bytes
stateRoot	String	The root of the final state trie of the block
timestamp	Number	The unix timestamp for when the block was collated
totalDifficulty	String	Integer indicating the total difficulty of the chain until this block
transactions	Array	Array of transactions included in this block
transactionsRoot	String	The root of the transaction trie of the block (i.e., requests)
uncles	Array	Array of uncle hashes (i.e., orphan blocks that are not part of the longest chain)

contain any transactions (i.e., the transactions array field was empty). Next, we will
look at how to find the block that contains the transaction we are looking for.

4. **Finding Transactions**

Of course, we are interested in looking at the contents of the block that contains our
transaction. For this, we need first find out which block contains our transaction.
We can do this using the `eth.getTransaction` function, as well as the
transaction hash that was created when we specified the transaction.

The transaction hash was the value you received when you conducted your
transaction earlier in this exercise:

```
web3.eth.sendTransaction
(
    {
        from:personal.listAccounts[0],

        to:personal.listAccounts[2],

        value:1000
    }
);

"0x45b85025de231fd7641d475f0144bc130433cd843ea0190ac985b4734f889aa8"
```

You can now retrieve the block number corresponding to this transaction hash
by plugging it into the `eth.getTransaction` function:

```
> eth.getTransaction("0xac0ffcdcefdff5ace2940c67b04c07a345082397c5eba18a1499a491d64c53bb")
{
  blockHash: "0xfaf5a13a3c5f8fb58ae324cda93eee5790b4d86a9cbdcda146ac6ada02d1f247",
  blockNumber: 194,
  from: "0xe9c51fb5f23321142ee20e991413b956e1c5fbc6",
  gas: 90000,
  gasPrice: 1000000000,
  hash: "0x45b85025de231fd7641d475f0144bc130433cd843ea0190ac985b4734f889aa8",
  input: "0x",
  nonce: 0,
  r: "0xf289cc2cd78b4747b4cc28286551b6fdc0268d40781deb11d702828b372f0d8c",
  s: "0xa27f711d8db93dc26cef44b2640d6edc550f2949f3d9231df137f454315bd8",
  to: "0x24d016d3968facdf2c7f2c074522f1b92ce9ec30",
  transactionIndex: 0,
  v: "0xee",
  value: 7
}
```

Thus, we know that, in this instance, our transaction was included in block
number 5.

As a last step of this exercise, access the data of the block that contains the
transaction that you executed earlier via `web3.eth.getBlock`:

```
> web3.eth.getBlock(5)
{
    difficulty: 463544,
    extraData: "0xd88301081584676574688676f312e31312e34856c696e7578",
    gasLimit: 5679516,
    gasUsed: 21000,
    hash: "0xfaf5a13a3c5f8fb58ae324cda93eee5790b4d86a9cbdcda146ac6ada02d1f247",
    logsBloom:
"0x00000000000000000000000000000000000000000000000000000000000000000000000000000000
00000000000000000000000000000000000000000000000000000000000000000000000000000000000
00000000000000000000000000000000000000000000000000000000000000000000000000000000000
00000000000000000000000000000000000000000000000000000000000000000000000000000000000
00000000000000000000000000000000000000000000000000000000000000000000000000000000000
000000000000000000000000000000000000000000000000000000000000",
    miner: "0xe9c51fb5f23321142ee20e991413b956e1c5fbc6",
    mixHash: "0x9427ef16b1eb0c43668e4c17bde2a550e130b9007eaf97f494db302f1305c0eb",
    nonce: "0x237a365de59b3c2c",
    number: 194,
    parentHash: "0xeafc503df69623cf2827304e3013072fe9a7abfe851e3c6cc88f7309fa7fba40",
    receiptsRoot: "0x056b23fbba480696b65fe5a59b8f2148a1299103c4f57df839233af2cf4ca2d2",
    sha3Uncles: "0x1dcc4de8dec75d7aab85b567b6ccd41ad312451b948a7413f0a142fd40d49347",
    size: 642,
    stateRoot: "0x8b0ef92bf3b07e5baafbdc062c3fdda7988f0bd12a5cb3fa29595b1e59db1c18",
    timestamp: 1568542133,
    totalDifficulty: 99133622,
    transactions: ["0xac0ffcdcefdff5ace2940c67b04c07a345082397c5eba18a1499a491d64c53bb"],
    transactionsRoot:
"0xc126072514af52fa0f81eea33b37174b89a113153daddeb23bd501dadd86a0ae",
    uncles: []
}
```

As you can see from the example above, it is relatively simple to trace individual transactions to their origin. Similarly, by looking at the block data and the individual transaction data, you can "follow the money," that is determine from where funds used in a given transaction originated.

References

1. Tapscott A, Tapscott D (2018) Blockchain revolution: how the technology behind bitcoin and other cryptocurrencies is changing the world. Penguin, New York City
2. Brunton F (2019) Digital cash: the unknown history of the anarchists, utopians, and technologists who created cryptocurrency. Princeton University Press, Princeton
3. Casey M, Vigna P (2019) The truth machine: the blockchain and the future of everything. Picador, New York City
4. Bartlett J (2016) The dark net: inside the digital underworld. Melville House, Brooklyn
5. Tobias B (2014) Modern censorship: blocking access to the Tor network. AV Akademik-erverlag, Riga
6. Bair J, Shavers B (2016) Hiding behind the keyboard. Elsevier Science, Amsterdam
7. Narayanan A, Bonneau J, Felten E et al (2016) Bitcoin and cryptocurrency technologies: a comprehensive introduction. Princeton University Press, Princeton
8. Rosen A (2010) Concurrent zero-knowledge. Springer, Berlin
9. Yuan M (2020) Building blockchain apps. Addison-Wesley, Boston
10. Sherif M (2018) Protocols for secure electronic commerce. CRC Press, Boca Raton

Blockchain Cryptography: Part 1

6

6.1 Introduction

6.1.1 Cryptography Fundamentals

Cryptology is the science of encrypting and decrypting information and the methods employed to those ends. Cryptography (from the Greek "kryptós" (secret, hidden) and "gráphein" (writing) is a subset of cryptology that describes the creation of methods for encrypting information so it cannot be understood by unauthorized parties. Steganography refers to methods for disguising the communication channel over which cryptographically encrypted messages are sent. Cryptanalysis, another important sub-discipline of cryptology, is concerned with methods for decrypting cryptographically encrypted information without the consent of the party that encrypted the original message. Therefore, while a cryptographer changes information so it appears incomprehensible, the cryptanalyst renders this information comprehensible again, usually without permission.

Our desire to communicate secretively and the need to devise encryption methods to ensure sub rosa communication can be traced to ancient Egypt and Mesopotamia, with Hebrew scholars making the first serious attempts to use simple substitution ciphers around 600 BC (Sect. 6.2.1). Cryptographic methods play a crucial role in ensuring the proper operations of any blockchain system, but none of these early techniques, of course, provide enough security in today's computer age. This chapter provides a comprehensive overview of both the cryptographic building blocks (e.g., "hashing") and the underlying algorithmic processes, that is, the public-key cryptography and digital signatures that are used today to ensure the high level of security and control that blockchain-based systems offer.

© Springer Nature Switzerland AG 2020   125
D. Hellwig et al., *Build Your Own Blockchain*, Management for Professionals,
https://doi.org/10.1007/978-3-030-40142-9_6

6.1.2 Secrecy Prerequisites

Cryptographic methods allow us to protect data and to transmit sensitive information while ensuring that it remains unintelligible to unauthorized users. For such methods to be effective, three conditions must be met:

1. **Confidentiality** requires that only authorized persons be able to decrypt and read encrypted information. For example, if Alice doesn't have time to withdraw money before going to a party, she can ask Bob to withdraw $50 from her account by giving him her debit card and sending him her encrypted PIN in reverse order, as previously agreed, via SMS. Because only Bob knows the key to decrypting the PIN, he is the only person who can decrypt it. Eve, who happens to be sitting next to Bob and reading the received SMS, cannot do much with the encrypted PIN, even if she somehow gets hold of Alice's debit card.
2. **Integrity** requires that the information transmitted remain unaltered, so Alice's PIN must remain unaltered when a cryptographic method is used to encrypt it; otherwise, the PIN would no longer be decryptable. Furthermore, no two PINs should result in the same encrypted PIN (see Sect. 6.4.4 for more details).
3. **Authenticity** requires that one be able to confirm that a message came from the stated sender. Therefore, it must be clear to Bob that Alice sent the text message with the PIN, and it should not be possible for a third person pretending to be Alice to send the SMS to Eve. This verification step must be performed in a way that prevents it from being denied or revoked in retrospect.

6.1.3 Blockchain and Cryptography

The fundamental operations of blockchain technology leverage state-of-the-art cryptographic encryption technologies. Blockchain technology uses two fundamental processes for its operations: information hashing and digital signatures. Chapter 1 described how, as part of the blockchain data-storage process, hashing converts transaction information in every block into a digest that serves as a point of reference for all future transactions. This process ensures that the information captured in that digest cannot be altered later. We consider the technical elements of this process in more detail in Sect. 6.4. Blockchains also leverage digital signatures via public-key cryptography, which relies on the use of two keys for encryption and decryption. We introduce this topic in Sect. 6.6 and explore it further in Chap. 7. When combined, the hashing and public-key cryptographic algorithms ensure that the three encryption principles of confidentiality, integrity, and authenticity are met and can be leveraged to enable the blockchain ecosystem (e.g., for cryptocurrencies).

Recall that, for Bitcoin, the core functional element is not to encrypt information but to create a digital fingerprint to control ownership, that is, to allow only the actual owner of any individual account to manage the Bitcoin funds associated with this account. Bitcoin uses the SHA256 algorithm to aggregate bitcoin transfers into hash blocks (Sect. 6.2.1). This algorithm pools transactions and stores them in a manner that is computationally expensive and challenging to replicate. If Bitcoin transactions were not encrypted in this way, anyone could change transactions as they pleased. In short, cryptocurrencies like Bitcoin could not exist in the absence of cryptographic encryption techniques.

This chapter provides the basics of cryptographic processes. Section 6.2 introduces the fundamentals of cryptography and its underlying motivation by focusing on the historic effort to exchange information while preventing others from accessing it (e.g., using ciphers to represent messages in ancient Rome). Section 6.3 introduces modern cryptographic algorithms and revisits some concepts that were introduced earlier in this book (e.g., hashing). Sections 6.6.2 and 6.6.3 then introduce two basic cryptographic methods as preparation for Chap. 7. Finally, Sect. 6.8 addresses the realm of post-quantum encryption, which originated from the acknowledgment that most cryptography implementations in use today can hypothetically be broken by sufficiently powerful quantum computers, as all of the underlying mathematical problems can be solved via quantum algorithms.

6.2   Classic Ciphers

Two of the more historically common methodological approaches for encrypting information were substitution and transposition. Substitution replaces individual letters of a message with other letters, numbers, or characters, while transposition methods mix the individual components of a message. Both approaches have several applications and implementations.

Perhaps the most famous examples of these methods are the Caesar cipher and the Scytale. The Caesar cipher is a substitution cipher named in honor of Julius Caesar, who allegedly used it to encrypt official messages [1]. Scytale is an ancient transposition cipher, commonly used in ancient Greece, that required the use of a cylinder around which a piece of paper with the message written on it was wrapped. To decrypt and read the message, the recipient used a cylinder of the same dimensions.

6.2.1   Substitution

Consider the following example: Suppose Alice wants to send Bob the message, "Meet me at ten." Since Alice does not want anyone other than Bob to read this message, she agrees with Bob to encrypt and decrypt messages according to the Caesar cipher.

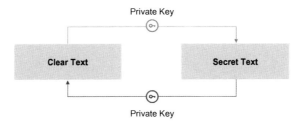

Fig. 6.1 Illustration of the substitution method

Using the formula "X = Y + 3," Alice inserts a letter of the original message (Y) into the formula by shifting the output X by three letters. This method turns an "A" into a "D," a "D" into a "G," and so on. If Bob wants to decrypt the message from Alice again, he must reverse the Caesar key, using the formula "Y = X − 3" (Fig. 6.1).

6.2.2 Transposition

Transposition ciphers encrypt the contents of a plaintext message by conversion (permutation) of individual characters or letters. The simplest transposition cipher consists of rearranging the letters of a message in groups, which in this example requires the use of the permutation 42513 (Fig. 6.2).

Transposition ciphers can usually be analyzed easily. For example, a letter frequency analysis can show an attacker whether an encryption is a transposition cipher, as the relative frequency of letters used in a language remains the same. Subsequently, from the analysis of certain strings, the order and number of columns can be determined. For example, the string "ein" is common in German, so the likely column order adjustments can be inferred. Similarly, if a message encrypted in German starts with an article (Fig. 6.2), it can only be "der," "die," or "das." In this example because of the existing vowels, it would have to be "die," so the fourth

Fig. 6.2 Simple
transposition

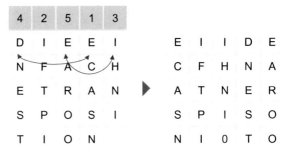

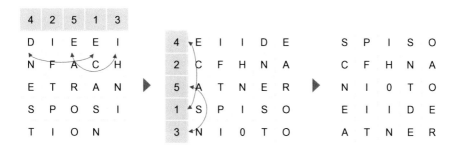

Fig. 6.3 Nihilist transposition

column is the first, and so on. An attacker can derive considerable information from the ciphertext itself, so with a little trial and error, these ciphers are easily broken.

An improvement on the encryption by means of transposition ciphers can be achieved by linking the column permutation with the line permutation, a method known as the Nihilist transposition (Fig. 6.3). In this procedure, both the columns and the lines are permuted. The ciphertext is then read according to the newly obtained (line) order.

6.3   Modern Cryptographic Algorithms

6.3.1   Introduction

Today, with unprecedented amounts of computing power available at a moment's notice, all classical encryption methods have been rendered obsolete. One encryption machine that epitomizes the turning point brought on by the emergence of the electronic computer was the Enigma machine, an electronic cipher machine used in the Second World War by the German military to transmit messages.

Initially, the Enigma machine was considered unbreakable, given approximately 15 quintillion (i.e., a fifteen with eighteen zeros) different configuration settings for the encryption process [2]. However, in 1940, the mathematician Alan Turing created mathematical calculations and theories that broke the Enigma system. Along with his team, Turing developed the "Turing Bomb," an electrical machine that decrypted the Enigma code. These "bombs" were up to two meters high and five meters wide and were the predecessors of our modern computers, leading Turing to be known as the father of the modern computer.

Algorithms in the field of cryptography can be divided into three major areas: Hashing algorithms, symmetric algorithms, and asymmetric algorithms. All cryptographic efforts preceding 1976 fall into the first category of systems that rely on one key for both encryption and decryption. A new class of cryptography arose when Diffie, Hellman, and Merkle (1976) introduced the concept of public-key cryptography (see Chap. 7 for more details). The main difference here was that one did not have to use the same key for decryption and encryption, as the key could be separated into two parts: one for encryption and one for decryption. This method can be used for both the identification of identities (digital signatures) and for traditional secret communication. This class of cryptographic protocols deals primarily with the establishment of secure communication channels by leveraging public-key cryptographic methods. Blockchain technology relies primarily on the concepts of hashing and digital signatures, the latter of which are enabled by asymmetric cryptographic algorithms.

What follows is a brief introduction to each of the three categories, highlighting the main differences among them. The subsequent sections provide a deep dive into the technicalities of each type of algorithm.

Hashing

The hashing mechanism is used primarily to transform large amounts of information into fixed-size pieces of data ("hashes") and is usually used for verification purposes (e.g., allowing Alice to prove to Bob that information existed at a given time without revealing the information) and so does not require a key (or password) in the classical sense. Section 6.4 provides a step-by-step explanation of what happens with the data to which we apply a hash function using the SHA-1 algorithm. While no longer used because of its vulnerabilities, this algorithm lends itself well to illustrating the steps in the process.

Symmetric Encryption

Symmetric key algorithms use individual keys to encrypt information. To allow Alice to send information to Bob, both must agree on a shared key beforehand. Because of blockchain's technical infrastructure, there is no real need for symmetric encryption; instead, all major currencies rely exclusively on asymmetric encryption methods that leverage the Elliptic Curve Digital Signature Algorithm (ECDSA). However, to make understanding the convoluted structure of these more advanced encryption methodologies easier, Chap. 7 lays out some of the cryptographic foundations by considering two symmetric encryption methods first.

Asymmetric Encryption

Asymmetric-key algorithms use two mathematically linked keys, one of which is used for decryption (to be retained by the creator of the keys) and the other for encryption (to be shared publicly). With asymmetric encryption, the two parties need not agree on a key beforehand to be able to communicate securely in the digital realm. In Chap. 7, we consider the most common mechanisms (called RSA and Elliptic Curve Cryptography, ECC) along with the implications of post-quantum cryptography for the world of cryptocurrencies. Table 6.1 summarizes the key attributes of the three types of algorithms.

Table 6.1 Differences among hashing, symmetric, and asymmetric algorithms

Feature	Hashing	Symmetric	Asymmetric
# of keys	0	1	2
Typical key size	–	256-bit	• RSA: 2048-bit • ECC: 256-bit
Typical algorithm	SHA	AES	RSA
Speed	Fast	Fast	Medium
Complexity	Low	Medium	High
Examples	SHA-1, SHA-2, etc.	AES, etc.	RSA, ECC, etc.
Use cases	• Digital signatures • Key derivation	• Message encryption • Storage encryption	• Digital signatures • Session keys

6.3.2 Vulnerabilities

Here we provide an overview of the most common attack vectors for ciphers and encryption methods. These methods are introduced up front, as they are useful in explaining and analyzing the logic behind the various cipher methods.

- **Brute-force attacks**: In this kind of attack, all possible keys are tried, one after the other, although the order may be based on their probability of success. For example, many people use special dates as their passwords, making such passwords more likely, and it takes less than a second to try all possible date combinations that have occurred in the past 100 years. This method is also effective if the use of a relatively weak password can be assumed. Even using only commercially available computers, tens of millions of keys per second can easily be tried.
- **Ciphertext-only attacks**: In a ciphertext-only attack (COA), or known ciphertext attack for cryptanalysis, the attacker has access only to a set of ciphertexts based on which the attacker attempts to reconstruct the original message (e.g., by letter-frequency analyses to determine what encrypted words might correspond to the plaintext words).
- **Known plaintext attacks**: In a Known Plaintext Attack (KPA), the attacker knows parts of the transmitted plaintext (also called the crib) and the encrypted version of the same text (ciphertext). Based on these two elements, the attacker attempts to derive the secret key.

6.4 Hashing

6.4.1 Introduction

In modern computer-aided cryptography, especially in blockchain technology, algorithms are used to encrypt information. The information that must be encrypted in the Bitcoin blockchain is transaction information.

Suppose Alice transfers a bitcoin from her bitcoin wallet to Bob's bitcoin wallet. This transaction is now recognized by the Bitcoin nodes. If several nodes conclude that the transaction has taken place correctly and has followed all the rules, the node operators will integrate the transaction into a hash block and, thus, also into the blockchain.

If even a single character of the original message is changed, the result is altered completely. Compare the result when the name is altered from "Sasha" to "Masha":

- SHA256 ("The quick brown fox jumps over the lazy dog Sasha")
  dd517ac8a8c16b4e4e7c505a34213e3b24c2a211ef71e2c1284366c518994d4a
- SHA256 ("The quick brown fox jumps over the lazy dog Masha")
  e1005ba6d9a78c482b65bc9287085f46a9bea8e8efcf3ad74e28ec430541eb8f.

The same is true when applied to transaction data and blocks, which is important because the hash value of a block reveals whether the data from a previous transaction has been tampered with or has already been included in a previous block ("double spending"). In both cases, all other blockchain nodes will disregard the manipulated blocks, as the manipulation can easily be identified, so these fraudulent blocks will never become part of the blockchain.

To function as expected, the SHA256 algorithm must be able to combine into one hexadecimal number several pieces of information, such as information about the sender, the receiver, the transaction amount, a timestamp, and block metadata.

Next, we discuss the vulnerabilities of hashing algorithms—mainly the notion of "collisions." The emergence of collisions rendered once widely adopted hashing algorithms insecure and unusable. For example, the SHA-1 algorithm, which we review in detail in Sect. 6.5, was put out of use when researchers at Google identified hashing collisions.

6.4.2 Hash Collisions

For any hash function, a collision occurs if there are two inputs, x_1 and x_2, such that their respective hash values are equivalent (i.e., $h(x_1) = h(x_2)$), as depicted in Fig. 6.4.

For two primary reasons, collisions produced by any hash function have profound effects on the function's security: First, if two input messages produce the same hash, it is likely that the hash space is not evenly distributed. For example, for a 256-bit hash, we would expect to have to hash 2^{128} messages before finding a collision with a probability of approximately 40 percent. Second, if a collision can be predicted or guessed easily, forging a message that leads to the same hash is no longer a challenge, thereby allowing attacks (e.g., a second pre-image attack).

To have a 50 percent chance at finding a hash collision, one needs at least 4×10^{38} attempts. Or, stated differently, if one had tried a trillion messages every second since the beginning of the universe, it would still take 787 million times longer to have a 40 percent chance at finding a collision.

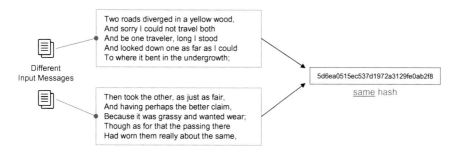

Fig. 6.4 Illustration of a hash collision

$$\frac{2^{128}}{(1.37 \times 10^9) * (365 * 24 * 60 * 60) * (10^{12})} \approx 7.87 \times 10^8$$

Thus, with a hash function, we want to ensure that it (1) samples from the result spaces uniformly (i.e., any hash output is equally probable), (2) is resistant to guessing an input from an output (preimage resistance), and (3) given an input, it is resistant to guessing another input that produces the same hash as the first (i.e., second preimage resistance). These three properties are interdependent.

6.4.3 Merkle-Damgård Construction

The Merkle-Damgård construction, which is the basic construction of most of today's crypto-hash functions, was derived independently by two researchers, Ralph Merkle and Ivan Damgård [3]. In this construction, the input message is subdivided into individual, equally long blocks m_1, m_2, ..., m_n; the last block is filled by padding. The exact block length and padding rule are subject to the design parameters of the hash function (e.g., SHA-1, which we introduce in Sect. 6.5). These individual message blocks are then processed sequentially with a compression function f.

6.4.4 Length Extension Attack

A length extension attack is possible only if a hash function operates on fixed-sized blocks (like SHA-1 and SHA-2). A non-complete block is padded with values that depend only on the length of the message. (For example, every two-byte message uses the same padding bits to complete one block.) This message-padding design principle can be exploited if an attacker replaces part of the padding with additional message content. Since the secret is at the beginning of the message, it will not be affected by the changes to the message length and padding.

In practice, once found, a collision (e.g., of a 512-bit block) can be extended (front and back) by more data blocks:

$$M_0, M_1, \ldots, M_i, \ldots, M_n$$
$$M_0, M_1, \ldots, N_i, \ldots, M_n$$

If the (intermediate) hash value is the same for the data blocks $M_i \neq N_i$, then it does not change with any subsequent data blocks, assuming these subsequent blocks are equal. The implications can be profound. Consider document verification as an example: An arbitrary document can be signed (i.e., the hash can be generated) and the content subsequently extended without impacting the resulting hash value.

One can think about this is by considering a protocol that specifies a secret word (e.g., "banana") that will be used to indicate the start of a message (e.g., "attack at seven"). The "banana" prefix indicates that the sender is authentic. With a length-extension attack, the initial message might have been sent (i.e., "banana attack at seven"), but a malicious third-party attacker can just continue to add to this message (e.g., "… and fifty minutes from left flank"), and the recipient will still think the message is verified, given the "banana" prefix. To counteract the possibility of such an attack, it is safer to include the secret word, followed by the number of words in the message (i.e., "banana three attack at seven"); in this manner, the receiver will know whether any extra words have been included.

A more relatable example is that of cash checks: Check-writers should always write "—— 10,000.00" and "ten thousand ——" to prevent someone from changing the amount on a (signed) check to another value (e.g., "110,000.00" and "one hundred ten thousand," which could also be considered a length extension attack.

Length-extension attacks are highly effective against naïve, e.g., hash (secret ‖ message), hash-based message-authentication code (MAC) constructs, that act like a symmetric signature, where the same secret key is used to create and to verify the signature (i.e., the message authentication code).

6.5 Secure Hash Algorithm (SHA)

6.5.1 Introduction

The SHA algorithm provides an early example of a standard hashing algorithm [4]. It was first published in 1993, jointly created by the National Security Agency (NSA) and the National Institute of Standards and Technology (NIST). The process works for any information input that is smaller than 2^{64} bits, which are billions of characters, and will always produce an output (digest, hash) that is exactly 160 bits long (i.e., 40 digits). The tenets for any hash function are that it be impossible to:

- go from the output back to the original message.
- find two different messages that produce the same output.

The hash value ensures the integrity of a message. To that end, the hash function must be collision-proof; that is, it must be impossible to create two different input messages with the same hash value output (as introduced in Sect. 6.4.2).

In theory, several strings must ultimately result in the same hash, given the hash digest is of finite length, regardless of the input data. However, the hash algorithm must make the occurence of such collisions as difficult as possible. For any hash function, the smallest changes in the plain text or message inputs should result in large changes in the hash value.

The next section explains how the SHA-1 hashing algorithm works in practice. Given the length of the procedure, the examples cannot be too comprehensive, but we provide pseudo-code and an indication of what is happening during each step.

6.5.2 Hash Example

Step 1: Split the input text into an array of the character's ASCII codes (i.e., "Blockchain" becomes [B,l,o,c,k,c,h,a,i,n]), which then becomes:
`[66,108,111,99,107,99,104,97,105,110]`

Step 2: Convert the ASCII codes into binary format:
`[1000100, 1101100, 1101111, 1100011, 1101011, 1100011, 1101000, 1100001, 1101001, 1101110]`

Step 3: Pad zeros at the front of each of the characters to ensure that each is 8 bits long:

`[01000100,   01101100,   01101111,   01100011,   01101011, 01100011, 01101000, 01100001, 01101001, 01101110]`

Step 4: Concatenate the binary numbers, along with an extra 1:
`0100010001101100011011110110001101101011011000110110100001101101` `0000110000101101001011011101`

Step 5: Pad the binary message with zeros until its length becomes 512 mod 448; the padding ensures that the input is divisible by 512. (The output of SHA-1 will always be 40 bits long.) In our example, the concatenated string is 81 characters long, so we append 431 zeros.

Step 6: Determine the length of the 8-bit ASCII code array (step 3) and convert that to binary (i.e., 80), which is 1010000.

Step 7: Pad this array with zeros at the front until it is 64 characters long. (We add 57 zeros at the front.)

Step 8: Append the output from step 7 to the output from step 5. Since we are dividing the binary message by 512, the size of the input does not matter.

Step 9: Break the message into an array of 512-character parts for further processing, and break each 512-character piece into a subarray of sixteen 32-bit words.

Step 10: Loop through each array piece of the sixteen 32-bit words and extend each array to 80 words using bitwise operations, as defined by the SHA-1 protocol.

Step 11: Initialize variables h_1, h_2, h_3, h_4, and h_5.

Step 12: Loop through the pieces and perform (1) bitwise operations and (2) variable re-assignments (which changes the variables initialized in step 12), based on the specifications of the SHA-1 algorithm. This step ensures that the output will always be 40 bits: the SHA-1 function manipulates these five variables based on the length and composition of the arbitrary input message.

Step 13: After the loop process completes, the current state of the binary variables (h_1, h_2, h_3, h_4, and h_5) will be converted to hexadecimals again:

h_1 = 1111 0100 0101 1101 1000 1110 1110 0011 → EFE3FBAA
h_2 = 0110 1101 1011 0011 1111 0100 0011 1100 → 6DB3F43C
h_3 = 1111 0100 0101 1101 1000 1110 1110 0011 → F45D8EE3
h_4 = 1111 1101 1011 0001 0110 1000 1100 1101 → FDB168CD
h_5 = 0100 0100 1000 1010 1111 1010 0100 0001 → 448AFA41

Step 14: The resulting hexadecimal values can be joined together, resulting in the hashing output or digest of the "Blockchain" string input, based on the SHA-1 algorithm:
EFE3FBAA6DB3F43CF45D8EE3FDB168CD448AFA41

6.6 Symmetric Encryption

6.6.1 Single Encryption Keys

The principle of symmetric encryption is simple: Only one key is needed for both encryption and decryption, so both the sender and the receiver need the same key (Fig. 6.5). This requirement is not a problem for the sender since the sender already has the key for encryption, but a secure transmission path must be determined to forward the key to the receiver. In the past, this key was usually given to the receiver by a messenger.

Fig. 6.5 Symmetric encryption

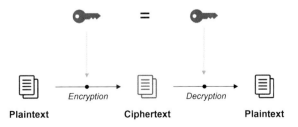

Plaintext   Encryption   Ciphertext   Decryption   Plaintext

Symmetric encryption is often used today, but since the transfer of the key is cumbersome, the principle of hybrid encryption has become an attractive alternative. This hybrid approach relies on asymmetric encryption for the symmetric key (Chap. 7) and symmetric encryption for the transfer of the actual data. The symmetric key is exchanged via a (slightly slower) asymmetric encryption approach, and subsequent communication is encrypted via (faster) symmetric encryption.

Symmetric encryption methods are divided into stream ciphers and block ciphers. With stream ciphers, the plaintext is encrypted or decrypted character by character; for block ciphers, as the name implies, plaintext is divided into fixed-size (e.g., 256-bit) blocks so multiple characters are encrypted or decrypted in one step.

We saw a couple of examples of the stream ciphers at the beginning of this chapter (the Caesar and transposition ciphers discussed in Sect. 6.2). Next, we will consider the Hill Cipher, a classic encryption method invented in 1929 by Lester S. Hill. The Hill cipher is the most general of the linear block ciphers that leverage matrices and will serve as a foundational example as we move toward modern cryptography.

6.6.2   The Hill Cipher

The Hill Cipher is a polygraphic cipher, meaning that the process can bundle more than a single letter at a time before encrypting the message. The Hill Cipher is based on linear algebra and modular division [5]. For encryption, the key is written to an n × n matrix, with which n characters of the ciphertext are repeatedly encrypted. Ciphertexts whose length is not divisible by n are padded with x. The padding x is then removed during decryption.

For decryption, an inverse matrix of the key matrix is computed. The set of available keys depends on common divisors, so alphabetical lengths that correspond to a prime are ideally suited. The key lengths must correspond to the squares of the matrix, making key lengths of 4 (2 × 2), 9 (3 × 3), 16 (4 × 4), and 25 (5 × 5) ideal. Note that computing an inverse matrix is not always possible.

The process for determining the number of suitable keys (i.e., with determinant 1) for the Hill Cipher is complicated: A block size of 2 has approximately 45,000 keys, and a block size of 3 has approximately 52 million keys. Therefore, a traditional brute-force attack becomes infeasible rather quickly as the block size increases. What follows is a step-by-step example of a plaintext encryption process that leverages the Hill Cipher method.

Step 1: Determine the edge length of the square key matrix that is used by taking the edge that can be mapped with the length of the key. We use the password BCIEELIJB for our encryption key matrix and code the letters of the plaintext and key in numbers, where: A = 0, B = 1, …, Z = 25.

$$K = \begin{pmatrix} B & E & I \\ C & E & J \\ I & L & B \end{pmatrix} = \begin{pmatrix} 1 & 4 & 8 \\ 2 & 4 & 9 \\ 8 & 11 & 1 \end{pmatrix}$$

The cipher will work only if the greatest common divisor of the determinant of the key matrix K and 26 is 1, because only then will the determinant have a multiplicative inverse that can be used both to decrypt and encrypt the plaintext.

Step 2: Pad the plain text with X letters at the end until it is divisible by the edge length. Consider the following text as a plaintext example:

Plaintext	B	L	O	C	K	C	H	A	I	N	B	O	O	K	W	H	U	X

This example plaintext has 17 characters. Because it is missing an additional character to be divisible by 3, X letters are added ("padded") at the end in our example. Then the letters of plaintext and key are coded in numbers, where: $A = 0$, $B = 1, \ldots, Z = 25$.

Plaintext	B	L	O	C	K	C	H	A	I	N	B	O	O	K	W	H	U	X
Position	1	11	14	2	10	2	7	0	8	13	1	14	14	10	22	7	20	23

Different letters can be mapped to different numbers depending on the block size chosen. However, in this example, mapping is one-to-one, as we are using a single block size.

Step 3: Write the plaintext into a matrix format in accordance with the edge length of the key matrix K that we selected in step 1:

$$P = \begin{pmatrix} 1 & 2 & 7 & 13 & 14 & 7 \\ 11 & 10 & 0 & 1 & 10 & 20 \\ 14 & 2 & 8 & 14 & 22 & 23 \end{pmatrix}$$

Step 4: Multiply the key matrix K by the plaintext matrix P.

$$K \cdot P = \begin{pmatrix} 1 & 2 & 8 \\ 4 & 4 & 11 \\ 8 & 9 & 1 \end{pmatrix} \cdot \begin{pmatrix} 1 & 2 & 7 & 13 & 14 & 7 \\ 11 & 10 & 0 & 1 & 10 & 20 \\ 14 & 2 & 8 & 14 & 22 & 23 \end{pmatrix}$$
$$= \begin{pmatrix} 135 & 38 & 71 & 127 & 210 & 231 \\ 202 & 70 & 116 & 210 & 338 & 361 \\ 121 & 108 & 64 & 127 & 224 & 259 \end{pmatrix}$$

The resulting matrix is modulo 26:

$$
\begin{pmatrix}
135 & 38 & 71 & 127 & 210 & 55 \\
202 & 70 & 116 & 210 & 338 & 119 \\
121 & 108 & 64 & 127 & 224 & 237
\end{pmatrix} \mod (26)
$$

$$
\rightarrow
\begin{pmatrix}
5 & 12 & 19 & 23 & 2 & 23 \\
20 & 18 & 12 & 2 & 0 & 23 \\
17 & 4 & 12 & 23 & 16 & 25
\end{pmatrix}
$$

Step 5: Convert the resulting numbers back to letters, resulting in the ciphertext:

Letter Position	5	20	17	12	18	4	19	12	12	23	2	23	2	0	16	23	23	25
Ciphertext	F	U	R	M	S	E	T	M	M	X	C	X	C	A	Q	X	X	Z

Decryption Process

For decryption, the matrix from the key is inverted and is multiplied by the matrix of the cipher modulo 26. The resulting numbers are then converted into letters to restore the plaintext.

Step 1: Invert the key matrix K that was chosen in Step 1 of the encryption process. The determinant of the key matrix must be 1 to ensure that there is a multiplicative inverse for the matrix. We calculate the inverse of K as follows:

$$K^{-1} = d^{-1} * adj(K)$$

To invert the encryption key matrix K, we must find the multiplicative inverse of the determinant of K, but first we calculate the determinant of K as:

$$
d = \begin{vmatrix}
a_1 & b_1 & c_1 \\
a_2 & b_2 & c_2 \\
a_3 & b_3 & c_3
\end{vmatrix}
= a_1 * \begin{vmatrix} b_2 & c_2 \\ b_3 & c_3 \end{vmatrix}
- b_1 * \begin{vmatrix} a_2 & c_2 \\ a_3 & c_3 \end{vmatrix}
+ c_1 * \begin{vmatrix} a_2 & b_2 \\ a_3 & b_3 \end{vmatrix}
$$

$$
d(K) = \begin{vmatrix}
1 & 2 & 8 \\
4 & 4 & 11 \\
8 & 9 & 1
\end{vmatrix}
= 1 * \begin{vmatrix} 4 & 11 \\ 9 & 1 \end{vmatrix}
- 2 * \begin{vmatrix} 4 & 11 \\ 8 & 1 \end{vmatrix}
+ 8 * \begin{vmatrix} 4 & 4 \\ 8 & 9 \end{vmatrix}
$$

$$d = 1$$

We must also find the adjunct matrix of K;

$$adj\begin{pmatrix} a_1 & b_1 & c_1 \\ a_2 & b_2 & c_2 \\ a_3 & b_3 & c_3 \end{pmatrix} = \begin{pmatrix} +\begin{vmatrix} b_2 & c_2 \\ b_3 & c_3 \end{vmatrix} & -\begin{vmatrix} b_1 & c_1 \\ b_3 & c_3 \end{vmatrix} & +\begin{vmatrix} b_1 & c_1 \\ b_2 & c_2 \end{vmatrix} \\ -\begin{vmatrix} a_2 & c_2 \\ a_3 & c_3 \end{vmatrix} & +\begin{vmatrix} a_1 & c_1 \\ a_3 & c_3 \end{vmatrix} & -\begin{vmatrix} a_1 & c_1 \\ a_2 & c_2 \end{vmatrix} \\ +\begin{vmatrix} a_2 & b_2 \\ a_3 & b_3 \end{vmatrix} & -\begin{vmatrix} a_1 & b_1 \\ a_3 & b_3 \end{vmatrix} & +\begin{vmatrix} a_1 & b_1 \\ a_2 & b_2 \end{vmatrix} \end{pmatrix}$$

$$adj(K) = adj\begin{pmatrix} 1 & 2 & 8 \\ 4 & 4 & 11 \\ 8 & 9 & 1 \end{pmatrix} = \begin{pmatrix} +\begin{vmatrix} 4 & 11 \\ 9 & 1 \end{vmatrix} & -\begin{vmatrix} 2 & 8 \\ 9 & 1 \end{vmatrix} & +\begin{vmatrix} 2 & 8 \\ 4 & 11 \end{vmatrix} \\ -\begin{vmatrix} 4 & 11 \\ 8 & 1 \end{vmatrix} & +\begin{vmatrix} 1 & 8 \\ 8 & 1 \end{vmatrix} & -\begin{vmatrix} 1 & 8 \\ 4 & 11 \end{vmatrix} \\ +\begin{vmatrix} 4 & 4 \\ 8 & 9 \end{vmatrix} & -\begin{vmatrix} 1 & 2 \\ 8 & 9 \end{vmatrix} & +\begin{vmatrix} 1 & 2 \\ 4 & 4 \end{vmatrix} \end{pmatrix}$$

$$adj(K) = \begin{pmatrix} -95 & 70 & -10 \\ 84 & -63 & 21 \\ 4 & 7 & -4 \end{pmatrix}$$

Step 2: Multiply the adjoint matrix of K with the ciphertext matrix:

$$K^{-1} = \begin{pmatrix} -95 & 70 & -10 \\ 84 & -63 & 21 \\ 4 & 7 & -4 \end{pmatrix} * \begin{pmatrix} 5 & 12 & 19 & 23 & 2 & 23 \\ 20 & 18 & 12 & 2 & 0 & 23 \\ 17 & 4 & 12 & 23 & 16 & 25 \end{pmatrix}$$

$$= \begin{pmatrix} 755 & 80 & -1085 & -2275 & -350 & -825 \\ -483 & -42 & 1092 & 2289 & 504 & 1008 \\ 92 & 158 & 112 & 14 & -56 & 153 \end{pmatrix}$$

Step 3: Divide K^{-1} modulo 26, which results in a matrix with the letter positions of the original decrypted input plaintext P:

$$P = \begin{pmatrix} 755 & 80 & -1085 & -2275 & -350 & -825 \\ -483 & -42 & 1092 & 2289 & 504 & 1008 \\ 92 & 158 & 112 & 14 & -56 & 153 \end{pmatrix} \mod (26)$$

$$= \begin{pmatrix} 1 & 2 & 7 & 13 & 14 & 7 \\ 11 & 10 & 0 & 1 & 10 & 20 \\ 14 & 2 & 8 & 14 & 22 & 23 \end{pmatrix}$$

The Hill Cipher has never been widely used, as mechanical encryption devices focused more on the use of polyalphabetic substitution [6]. With the emergence of digital computer technology, Hill's underlying concept of encryption, which is based on systems of equations, has re-emerged. However, even with less sophisticated digital computing technology, the Hill Cipher approach was still highly vulnerable to a known-plaintext attack. If one knows the plaintext and corresponding ciphertext, the key can be recovered because the encryption process is linear.

With the emergence of ever more powerful computers in the 1990s, a new type of cipher was needed that was based on mathematics that computers were not good at solving. This brings us to the discrete logarithm problem, which we introduce as part of the discussion of the Pohlig-Hellman cipher in Sect. 6.6.3.

Letter-frequency analysis does not work with this polygraphic cipher because the individual letters that form the plaintext input will not correspond to the same letter in the output. However, it is possible to track blocks: For example, a "da" in the plaintext will always map to the same two letters in the ciphertext. Hill created a mechanical machine that used block sizes of 6, but this machine was never widely used.

6.6.3 The Pohlig-Hellman Cipher

The Pohlig-Hellman exponentiation cipher provides a link between traditional and modern cryptographic methods [7]. This private (or symmetric) key cipher was proposed in 1976 but was not officially released until after the emergence of the Diffie-Hellman key exchange and the RSA cryptosystem.

The Pohlig-Hellman Cipher, a symmetric key cipher, is the logical successor to classic ciphers, as it shares key elements with other systems (e.g., shift ciphers like the Caesar cipher). However, Pohlig-Hellman also incorporates key elements from modern cryptography systems like RSA and Diffie-Hellman (e.g., DLP).

We will use the Pohlig-Hellman Cipher to introduce the concepts of the discrete logarithm problem and known-plaintext attacks without having to dive into the more complex ideas of public-key cryptography.

Example

Our motivation for introducing Pohlig-Hellman is to describe the process for the creating a ciphertext-only method that is resistant to known-plaintext-resistant attacks. For this example, we work with blocks of length 2 and divide our secret word, "blockchain," accordingly. We then convert all the resulting two-letter blocks into integers by concatenating the numbers for each letter (position in a 26-letter alphabet) (Table 6.1).

Plaintext	BL	OC	KC	HA	IN
Position	2.12	15.3	11.3	8.1	9.14
Combined	0212	1503	1103	0801	0914

To execute encryption and decryption using the Pohlig-Hellman Cipher, we choose a prime number that is larger than the largest possible block in our encryption space. For the example above, with a 26-letter alphabet, this number is 2626, so we need a prime number that is larger than that, say, 3001. We then need to choose a symmetric key, e, for use in the following encryption equation (where C is the ciphertext and P is the plaintext):

$$C \equiv P^e \bmod p$$

Assuming we choose e = 7, then:

$$(212)^7 \equiv 152 \bmod 3001$$
$$(1503)^7 \equiv 118 \bmod 3001$$
$$(1103)^7 \equiv 1741 \bmod 3001$$
$$(801)^7 \equiv 2998 \bmod 3001$$
$$(914)^7 \equiv 2337 \bmod 3001$$

As a result, we obtain the following ciphertext C:

Plaintext	BL	OC	KC	HA	IN
Position	2.12	15.3	11.3	8.1	9.14
Combined	0212	1503	1103	0801	0914
Encrypted	0152	0118	1741	2998	2337

The receiver of this ciphertext will decrypt it using nothing but the symmetric key that was previously shared. To do so, the recipient takes the corresponding eth roots of the ciphertext, which requires the inverse (i.e., a number d), such that:

$$C^d \equiv P \bmod p$$
$$(P^e)^d \equiv P \bmod p$$
$$P^{ed} \equiv P \bmod p$$
$$P^{ed}P^{-1} \equiv 1 \bmod p$$
$$P^{ed-1} \equiv 1 \bmod p$$

Therefore, to use the Pohlig-Hellman Cipher, one must know what numbers x $Px \equiv 1 \bmod p$ have. This is where Fermat's "Little Theorem" comes in: It states that, if p is a prime number, then for any integer a, the number a^p—a is an integer multiple of p.

In our example, as we selected p = 3001 and e = t, the greatest common denominator (GCD) of (e, p-1) is 1, so we can proceed with the decryption process. It follows that $d \equiv \bar{e} = 2143 \bmod 3000$, so:

$$(152)^{2143} \equiv 212 \mod 3001$$
$$(118)^{2143} \equiv 118 \mod 3001$$
$$(1741)^{2143} \equiv 1103 \mod 3001$$
$$(2998)^{2143} \equiv 801 \mod 3001$$
$$(2337)^{2143} \equiv 914 \mod 3001$$

One of the Pohlig-Hellman Cipher's key advantages over traditional ciphers is its protection against known-plaintext attacks. Any attacker who attempts a plaintext attack will have to solve the so-called discrete logarithm problem (DLP) by finding $e = \log_P C \mod p$. The fastest known algorithm for solving the DLP is significantly slower than the decryption mechanism that uses the symmetric key.

One approach to measuring the "goodness" of an encryption method is to determine how many keys there are, as this number forms the basis for a brute-force attack that tries all possible keys [8].

As we saw in the example above, "good" keys are derived by finding numbers between 1 and p-1 that share no factors with p-1. This number can be increased by choosing a large modulus or by electing larger block sizes of 3 or more letters.

For the cipher to be resistant to known-plaintext attacks, we must ensure that recovery of the key is mathematically more difficult than the processes of encryption and decryption. In our example, the key problem is to find a whole number e, such that $C \equiv P^e \mod p$; this problem, called the discrete logarithm problem (DLP), is a central element of all other cryptographic methods that we will consider.

Again, the key consideration here is the speed in which this mathematical problem can be solved. For example, if an attacker has some examples of P and C and wants to determine what e is, then he can multiply P by itself, modulo p, until he arrives at C. By keeping track of the number of multiplications, he determines e. This process is essentially the same as that followed for decryption, but if both parties who take part in the process know the factors of the exponent e beforehand, the process can be expedited.

Consider the following example: Suppose you want to calculate 2^{101}; this can be computed the obvious way (i.e., $2 * 2 * 2 * \cdots * 2$ repeated 101 times), but this approach requires 101 multiplication operations. However, if one can calculate $((2^{10})^{10}) * 2$ instead, the overall computational effort will be much smaller, as one can first calculate $2 * 2 * \cdots * 2$ ten times, resulting in 1024, followed by $1024 * 1024 * \cdots * 1024$ ten times, resulting in a total of $9 + 9 = 18$ operations. After that, the result must be multiplied by 2 once again, for a total of 19 individual multiplications, compared to 101 calculations performed the "normal" way.

The Pohlig-Hellman Cipher did not see broad adoption in the world of cryptography, primarily because it is slower than other private-key ciphers that are also able to resist known-plaintext attacks. The Pohlig-Hellman Cipher was not used in practice because of its low performance compared to other existing mechanisms at the time (e.g., AES, DES).

Summary

This chapter introduces the foundations of Blockchain cryptography using the hashing process and SHA-1 as examples. While this method is no longer widely used, it lends itself to illustrating the underlying principles of some of the newer methods (e.g., SHA-256) that are used today in the technical setup of Bitcoin and Ethereum. From a cryptography perspective, this chapter introduces the fundamentals necessary to comprehend the Blockchain-specific cryptographic mechanisms that we consider more closely in Chap. 7. While the various ciphers introduced here do not relate directly to the blockchain ecosystem, they are nonetheless critical parts of understanding the cryptographic mechanisms that build the technical foundation of today's blockchain realm.

6.7   Exercise

6.7.1   Introduction

The exercise for this chapter will require you to use the AES encryption method to send a message securely.

For simplicity, we use the same docker-based approach of launching a plain Ubuntu instance to work through the exercise, just as we did in the previous chapters.

Just as before, use the following command in the Windows console to download and start an interactive version of Ubuntu:

```
docker run -i -t --name aes ubuntu
```

Following this entry, you will see the following setup, which means that you are now in the command-line environment of a simulated Unix environment and you are ready to start the blockchain experiments. (Note that the string following the "root@" will be different from the example displayed below.)

```
root@<your-instance>:/#
```

6.7.2   Message Prep

First, create a simple text file containing the message that we want to encrypt. The content of the message in our example is shown below, but you can change the content of the text file to anything you like.

```
> echo "Attack at 5:00." > message.txt
```

Next, using the cat command, confirm that the contents of the message were stored correctly. The output should simply be the message that you entered in the first step:

```
> cat message.txt
Attack at 5:00.
```

6.7.3 OpenSSL Setup

Enter the following command to download the package lists from the repositories and update them:

```
apt-get update
```

Next, install the *openssl* component; this is a package that you will leverage to execute the symmetric encryption of your message.

Enter the following command to install openssl:

```
apt-get install openssl
```

6.7.4 Message Encryption

The openssl components supports various encryption standards. For your purposes, you can use the so-called Advanced Encryption Standard, or AES [9].

You can list the different cipher algorithms that are supported by openssl using the `openssl list -cipher-algorithms` following command:

```
> openssl list -cipher-algorithms
AES-128-CBC
AES-128-CBC-HMAC-SHA1
AES-128-CBC-HMAC-SHA256
...
SM4-CTR
SM4-ECB
SM4-OFB
```

Enter the following command in the console to initiate the encryption process:

```
> openssl enc -AES-256-CBC -base64 -in message.txt -out encrypted.txt -p -pass
pass:password
```

The output you receive should look like this:

```
salt=AA15A998CB50D436
key=D529A57CAC59A9BA00F8259E37B7247D93873E0DE9015484EFD6FC46FEF51AA2
iv =B50314AC17E166B81F52BA66089AAA8A
```

You get three items here: the salt, the key, and the initialization vector (IV).

The *salt* is used to ensure that the same password does not result in the same key. As you saw in the exercise and have seen in everyday life, the passwords you use can be short. From any password you use within OpenSSL, a key is generated that is then used to encrypt the actual data. As part of this process, the salt, a randomly generated value, is used to ensure that the same password does not result in the same key. The salt is not secret or randomly generated. If you were to work with keys directly, you would not need a salt value.

Next take a look at the *key*. As described above, the key is generated from the password that you select. This key (either 128bit or 256bit) is derived using a password-derivation function. The most commonly used function for this derivation is the so-called Password-Based Key Derivation Function 2 (PBKDF2), which is very slow by design. Why is that? It's because this makes launching a brute force attack impossible as it would take too long to execute.

Finally, take a look at the *initialization vector (IV)*. At this point, you have a key that was derived based on the password you chose. A problem could still arise if you happen to encrypt the same information twice, either in the same or in subsequent messages. As soon as you move to a block operation mode (i.e., you encrypt more data than can be contained in a single block), you will need to modify the message. Figure 6.6 depicts this process (i.e., cipher block chaining). The initialization vector is only used for the first block encryption; after that, the encrypted cipher text from the first block can be used (and so on…).

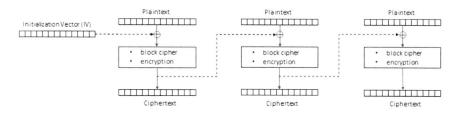

Fig. 6.6 Cipher block chaining (CBC)

For the first block, take the IV with the plain text; after that, use the encryption text (of block 1) for the subsequent blocks.

Next, look at the encrypted message, again using the cat command:

```
> cat encrypted.txt
U2FsdGVkX1+qFamYy1DUNiL5rX/a2gfIKSA6zv315hhzUFi1kWt/kY8Cr2SCPr+g
```

6.7.5 Message Decryption

Following the encryption, we want to decrypt our message again using the following command:

```
> openssl enc -AES-256-CBC -base64 -in encrypted.txt -out decrypted.txt -p -pass
pass:password -d

salt=AA15A998CB50D436
key=D529A57CAC59A9BA00F8259E37B7247D93873E0DE9015484EFD6FC46FEF51AA2
iv =B50314AC17E166B81F52BA66089AAA8A

> cat decrypted.txt
Attack at 5:00.
```

References

1. Holden J (2017) The mathematics of secrets: cryptography from caesar ciphers to digital encryption. Princeton University Press, Princeton
2. Kim D, Solomon M (2018) Fundamentals of information systems security. Jones & Bartlett Learning, Burlington
3. Paar C, Pelzl J (2011) Understanding cryptography: a textbook for students and practitioners. Springer, Heidelberg
4. Secure Hash Standard (SHS). https://nvlpubs.nist.gov/nistpubs/FIPS/NIST.FIPS.180-4.pdf

5. Lindell Y (2019) Tutorials on the foundations of cryptography. Springer, Cham
6. Klima R, Sigmon N (2012) Cryptology: classical and modern with maplets. Chapman & Hall/CRC, Boca Raton
7. Easttom C (2016) Modern cryptography: applied mathematics for encryption and information security. McGraw-Hill Education, New York City
8. Whitman M, Mattord H (2018) Principles of information security. Cengage Learning, Boston
9. (2001) Advanced Encryption Standard (AES). https://nvlpubs.nist.gov/nistpubs/FIPS/NIST. FIPS.197.pdf

Blockchain Cryptography: Part 2

7.1 Asymmetric Key Schemes

7.1.1 Introduction

Chapter 6 introduced the concept of symmetric cryptography. As the name suggests, a symmetric encryption scheme uses the same key for both encryption and decryption; the key is known to the sender and recipient of the message but must remain unknown to anyone else. To communicate

secretly, a sender uses an invertible cryptographic function to encrypt a plaintext m with the key k and then sends the resulting ciphertext c to the recipient. The recipient obtains the ciphertext c and uses the key k with the inverse function, there by recovering the plaintext m. The safest way for the sender and the recipient to exchange the key so it remains unknown to outsiders is via an in-person meeting, a feature that is a major weakness of symmetric encryption methods. The Caesar cipher introduced in Sect. 6.2. is an example of such a symmetric encryption method.

This hurdle related to exchanging keys securely became the motivating driver for developing asymmetric encryption, where such an exchange is no longer necessary because two keys are employed, one for encryption, and another for decryption. Here, each person has a public key and a private key (public-key cryptography); the public key is used to encrypt a message, and the private key is used to decrypt it. Since the public key owned by person A is publicly visible (e.g., included in an email signature), anyone can send a secure message to person A, but only person A can decrypt the message using his private key; therefore, the first function must not be reversible because, otherwise, anyone with the public key could reverse the function and unlock the secret message. Still, there must be a connection between the public and the private key functions or the intended recipient would not be able to decrypt the message. Thus, while the two keys are mathematically linked, an attacker should not be able to decipher the private key from the public key, a feature we consider in greater detail in Sect. 7.3.

© Springer Nature Switzerland AG 2020
149
D. Hellwig et al., *Build Your Own Blockchain*, Management for Professionals,
https://doi.org/10.1007/978-3-030-40142-9_7

In 1977, Ronald Rivest, Adi Shamir, and Leonard Adleman, two computer scientists and one mathematician, respectively, published the first general solution to the problem of asymmetric encryption, a cryptosystem known as RSA [1]. At that time, powerful symmetric key schemes existed, but the need for secure communication that did not require a shared secret to conduct the encryption and decryption processes had not yet been addressed.

The following sections first introduce the problem of asymmetric encryption, followed by an introduction to the Diffie-Hellman key exchange protocol, an asymmetric protocol published in 1976 that allows parties to exchange keys to be used for symmetric encryption schemes securely. Sections 7.3 and 7.4 introduce RSA and ECC, the most commonly used techniques for asymmetric encryption, both of which are critical to the Blockchain system.

7.1.2 Illustrative Example

The key difference between asymmetric and symmetric encryption is that asymmetric encryption uses two keys, one to encrypt (available to all) and one to decrypt (available only to the recipient) the message. The recipient must always pre-compute both keys and share the public portion in advance to allow potential senders to use the public key to encrypt messages for the recipient (Fig. 7.1).

Consider the following example: Alice and Bob want to send secret messages to each other using asymmetric cryptography. They do not need to be concerned with the security of the connection they will use to send their messages, even if all

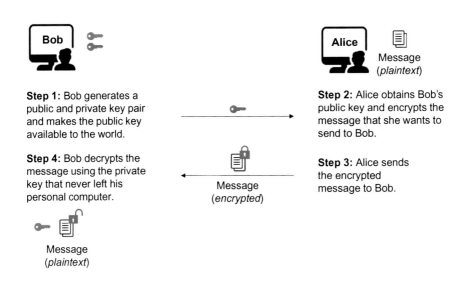

Fig. 7.1 Asymmetric encryption scheme

information sent via their computers is intercepted. To send a secure message to Bob, Alice first obtains Bob's public key (e.g., an alphanumeric string or file) that Bob may have posted on the internet or included in his email signature. Alice also has a public key, which Bob uses similarly to encrypt his return message to Alice. Alice then decrypts his answer using her private key. In summary, then, both Alice and Bob have private keys corresponding to their public keys: Alice and Bob generate their private/public key pairs on their respective computers, and the private key is never sent to anyone; it stays on their computers and is used only for the decryption process.

7.2   Diffie-Hellman-Merkle Key Agreement

7.2.1   Introduction

Diffie-Hellman-Merkle, an asymmetric, cryptographic technique used for key exchange or key agreement, was published in 1976 by the scientists Diffie, Hellman, and Merkle. Later, it was revealed that three scientists of the British secret service (GCHQ) had invented the principle of this procedure a few years earlier, but for reasons related to secrecy, it was not made public at the time, and these scientists were not credited for their work.

In practice, the Diffie-Hellman-Merkle key exchange protocol ensures that two or more communication partners agree on a common session key to be used for encryption and decryption. In typical cryptographic key-exchange techniques, the secret session key is exchanged during an initial negotiation phase between two communication partners so they can both encrypt and decrypt the data.

With the Diffie-Hellman-Merkle key exchange protocol, the secret session key itself is never transmitted; instead, only the result of an arithmetic operation is transmitted, which does not by itself allow an attacker to determine the key. In this arithmetic operation, one starts from the assumption that the exponentiation of numbers is easy but that calculating the discrete logarithm is difficult [2]. If the necessary computational power is lacking and no efficient solution for the discrete-logarithm problem exists, this procedure enables a secure key exchange. While it has become common to speak of a "key exchange," the term "key agreement" is more appropriate for Diffie-Hellman because the communication partners never actually *exchange* the secret session key; rather, they *agree* on a secret key.

The Diffie-Hellman-Merkle key exchange forms the basis for the Secure Shell protocols, SSH2 and OpenSSH, as well as IPSec and TLS with Forward Secrecy and Perfect Forward Secrecy [3]. However, because key exchange requires interaction between two parties, this method cannot be used to encrypt emails directly; instead, people rely on asymmetric cryptography like RSA (Sect. 7.3).

The next example shows the Diffie-Hellman-Merkle key exchange protocol at work.

7.2.2 An Example

Consider Alice and Bob, who want to encrypt their communication and so want to exchange the secret session key required for encryption and decryption in advance. To protect the session key from an attacker who may be intruding on their communications, they agree to use the Diffie-Hellman-Merkle key exchange (Fig. 7.2).

To that end, Alice and Bob agree on a large prime p, as well as a natural number q, which should be a generator of group Z (q). Both values may be known publicly, so they can be transmitted over an insecure channel. In this case, Alice chooses the numbers $p = 11$ and $q = 7$ for the key exchange.

Alice then generates a random number a, which must be smaller than the chosen prime number $p(1 \ldots p - 1)$. For this example, Alice chooses $a = 3$. Then Alice makes the following calculations:

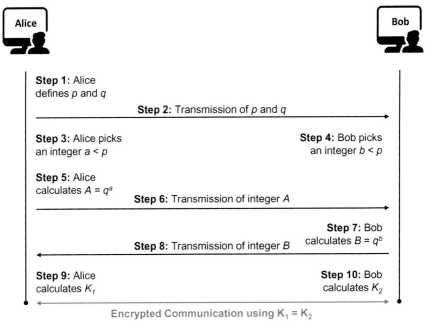

Fig. 7.2 Diffie-Hellman key exchange process

$$A = q^a \bmod (p)$$
$$A = 7^3 \bmod (11)$$
$$A = 2$$

Next, Alice transfers the numbers p and q and the result A to Bob. Since their communication might be subject to intermission, a potential attacker may know what p, q, and A are at this point.

Bob then generates another random number b that is smaller than the chosen prime $p(1 \ldots p - 1)$. He chooses b = 6 and then makes the following calculations to obtain his secret:

$$B = q^b \bmod (p)$$
$$B = 7^6 \bmod (11)$$
$$B = 4$$

Next, Bob transfers the result B back to Alice. Since the line of communication may be compromised, the attacker now may have knowledge of p, g, A, and B.

Alice now calculates the key K_1:

$$K_1 = B^a \bmod (p)$$
$$K_1 = 4^3 \bmod (11)$$
$$K_1 = 9$$

Similarly, Bob calculates another key, K_2:

$$K_2 = A^b \bmod (p)$$
$$K_2 = 2^6 \bmod (11)$$
$$K_2 = 9$$

Using this approach, both Alice and Bob will come to the same conclusion and, thus, have a common secret key that can be used as a temporary session key in a symmetric procedure:

$$K_1 = K_2$$

While the attacker knows p, g, A, and B, as all these values are transmitted as part of Alice and Bob's communication, the attacker can calculate the key K only if she knows a and b. Since these values are not transmitted, the attacker must calculate the key using other means, which is almost impossible to do with a sufficiently large prime input number. This problem is known as the discrete logarithm problem.

To illustrate the problem, consider the following example: Solving 3^{11} mod $(17) = x$ for x is relatively easy, even with larger numbers, but doing the opposite, that is, calculating the discrete logarithm based on the equation $11 = 3^x$ mod (17), is difficult, even with the computing technology available today.

7.2.3   Limitations

With Diffie-Hellman-Merkle and other discrete logarithm methods, a full key search is not the most effective attack method, but there are algorithms for calculating the discrete logarithm that, although nontrivial, are still faster than performing a full key search. Nonetheless, the larger the g, x, and y, the higher the computational effort and the greater the safety: A key length of 1024 bits is considered an absolute minimum, but 2048-bit keys or more are recommended.

A real danger is a so-called man-in-the-middle attack. The concept behind this attack is surprisingly simple and is not limited to computer security or online areas. In its simplest form, the attacker, Eve, sits between two parties, Alice and Bob, who communicate with each other. Eve listens to the messages sent and pretends to be one of the two parties. In the real world, Eve may send fake invoices to Alice, pretending to be Bob, and then simply intercept the checks that Alice sends back to Bob. In the online world, the attacks are slightly more complex, but the basics are the same. Eve intervenes between her victim and a resource that seeks to reach the victim. To be successful, Eve's presence must go undetected by both Alice and Bob. One solution to prevent a man-in-the-middle attack is to use digital signatures (Sect. 7.5.3): The danger is reduced by altering keys for various parts of the message, which requires that the communication partners work with alternating keys. Thus, even if the attacker obtains one of the keys, she can decrypt only part of the communication.

7.3   Rivest, Shamir, and Adelman (RSA)

7.3.1   Introduction

RSA is an asymmetric encryption method in the form of public-key cryptography, where an encryption key can be known to everyone, but only the person who has the private key can decrypt the message. RSA was the first published implementation of a public-private key encryption scheme.

After the publication of Diffie-Hellmann-Merkle, scientists wanted to find a trap-door, one-way function that could be reversed only if the receiver had the correct information. Consider Alice and Bob, who want to communicate securely while Eve intercepts and eavesdrops on their communication.

Alice creates a private key, uses it to generate a public key, and then shares the public key with everyone else, including her friend Bob and curious Eve. Such a public key must support the concept of a one-way function, so it is impossible for Eve to reverse the function and decrypt Bob's messages to Alice, which he encrypts using Alice's public key. Alice is the only one who can use her private key to decrypt the messages Bob sends.

The modulo function plays an important role in the asymmetric encryption of Rivest, as this function is irreversible. For example, in calculating 73,735 mod 23 = 20, the knowledge of the number 20 is not useful in finding the original number 73,735 since there are too many numbers that give the remainder 20 when they are divided by 23.

Next, we consider the detailed inner workings of the RSA process, provide some intuition for its "trap-door" functionality, and work through one numeric example to illustrate how RSA works in practice.

7.3.2 Key Pairs

The first step in the generation of a public-private key pair is to choose two large prime numbers, p and q. Both prime numbers should be of approximately equal size. The selection of the size of the prime numbers should correspond with the required level of security; that is, the product of p and q should be the desired key size (i.e., a number that when written as binary would be 1024, 2048 ... bits large). Next, we multiply p and q to determine n:

$$n = p * q$$

The next step of the key-generation process is to determine Euler's totient for both p and q, and then to multiply these two numbers together to find m. Euler's totient, $\varphi(x)$, describes the number of integers smaller than x that are co-prime to x. (Two numbers are considered co-prime if they share no common factors, that is, when 1 is the only positive integer that is a factor of both. For example, 21 and 22 are co-prime because the factors of 21 are 1, 3, 7 and 21, and the factors of 22 are 1, 2, 11, and 22.)

By multiplying the Euler totients (i.e., φ) of p and q, we derive a new composite number, m. It is mathematically difficult to determine Euler's totient for this composite number unless we know p and q because we know from Euler's totient function that, if we multiply two prime numbers together, the Euler's totient of that product is equivalent to the Euler's totients of each of the prime numbers that were multiplied. Thus, m is the Euler's totient of n:

$$m = (p - 1) * (q - 1)$$

The next step of the key-pair-generation process is to select another number, e, that is co-prime to m. The easiest way to find an integer that fulfills this condition is to select a prime number that is smaller than m and is not a factor of m.

The final step is to find one more number, d, that, when multiplied by e and modulo m, results in 1. Therefore, we want to find d, such that:

$$d * e \bmod (m) = 1.$$

At this point, we are ready to share the public key, which consists of e and n, with everyone. To encrypt any given plaintext message, we simply raise that message (converted into a numeric form) to the eth power and perform a modulo division by n:

$$C = M^e \bmod(n)$$

Similarly, to decrypt, we take the encrypted cipher text C, raise it to the dth power, and perform a modulo division by n:

$$M = C^d \bmod(n)$$

We now have both a public key and a private key:

- Public key (e, n)
- Private key (d, n).

As a result, the following calculations are relatively easy and computationally inexpensive:

- Encryption given a public key
- Decryption given a private key
- Computing d if both (1) e and (2) Euler's totient of n (i.e., $\varphi(n)$) are known
- Computing Euler's totient of n (i.e., $\varphi(n)$), if both p and q are known

The following calculations are difficult and computationally expensive:

- Computing Euler's totient of n (i.e., $\varphi(n)$) for an arbitrary number n
- Factoring an arbitrary number n

Since the public key contains only (e, n), the information the attacker has to derive d is insufficient. Euler's totient of n is required to derive d in a reasonable amount of time. However, if the factors of n are known (i.e., p and q in our example), it is easy to derive $\varphi(n)$, given Euler's totient function:

$$\varphi(n) = (p - 1) * (q - 1)$$

This computation is easy for the person who generates the keys in the first place, but the public, which does not have access to p and q, would first have to factor n to be able to use Euler's totient function and find $\varphi(n)$. This factoring operation is prohibitively difficult even with the most advanced computers.

7.3.3   Intuition

Given the scope of this introductory volume, our goal is to provide some intuition for the inverse nature of the potentiation operations—that is, encryption by raising a number to the eth power (mod n), and decryption by raising the encrypted result to the dth power (mod n).

We have already established that the encryption processes follow the first equation, $C = M^e \bmod(n)$, and that decryption follows $M = C^d \bmod(n)$. We start by substituting the first equation into the second, which yields $M = M^{e*d}\%n$. Using $d*e = 1 \bmod \varphi(n)$, we obtain $M^1\%n = M$. Note that the exponents d and e cancel each other out.

Readers might recall the process of factoring from high school mathematics and ask themselves whether it is possible to derive the private key by simply factoring the public key. This is possible, but as Sect. 7.3.2. shows, factoring large numbers is computationally expensive, mainly because there is no efficient algorithm for that purpose. RSA is flexible with regard to the key length used; 1024-bit, 2048-bit, 4096-bit, and even larger keys are in use today.

One bit can be 0 (zero) or 1 (one), so 2048 bits gives 2^{2048} distinct numbers. A decimal digit has ten possible values—0, 1, 2,..., 9—so to find the number of decimal digits needed to make 2^{2048} distinct numbers, we solve

$$2^{2048} = 10^n$$
$$2048 * \log_{10}(2) = n * \log_{10} 10$$
$$n = 2048 * \log_{10}(2)$$
$$n = 616.5$$

Thus, we know that, when represented in decimal format, a 2048-bit key is a number with 617 digits. To provide an idea of the magnitude of such a number, here is an example of a 2048-bit number:

```
509386197052962000004999421109352490000374439406941819000002073247594033
230000021201487742910100001654141246052090000076383121516811800000017778
162856722800000297219418198039000001802400621611440000061672291289812800
000140172387732771000008687463532723960000075795784237405500000696855741
502277000003244124188219770000058566161367290700000265171493689140000
988599226466803000000742855537375725000009336937673378330000054274404850
553700000406200656480439000008361377001093830000080717746710149700006
849356383876850000047895672935279200000757918759196159000070152086700
001200000205034438934078000004166652448937900000000
```

There is no limit to the keys that can be used. As traditional computers become more powerful, RSA can adopt larger key sizes to ensure that the factoring of keys remains unfeasible. Of potential concern in this context are quantum-based computing devices that may be able to factor numbers much faster than traditional computers can. We discuss this topic in more detail in Sect. 7.6.

Next, we work through an illustrative numeric example of the RSA algorithm.

7.3.4 An Example

Keep in mind that the following example is merely illustrative: For any security-relevant application of RSA, the key sizes would have to be much larger (i.e., 2048-bit and larger) (Sect. 7.3.4).

- Step 1: Select two prime numbers, such as p = 61 and q = 53.
- Step 2: Compute n = p * q (n = 61 * 53 = 3233).
- Step 3: Compute Euler's totient of the product of $\varphi(n) = (p-1) * (q-1)$ $(\varphi(3233) = (61-1) * (53-1) = 3120)$.
- Step 4: Chose any number e, such that 1 < e < 3120, that is also co-prime to 3120; in our case, we choose e = 17.
- Step 5: Determine d, the multiplicative inverse of e; following $d*e \bmod(n) = 1$, we derive that d is 2753.

Based on the example parameters selected above and following steps 1–5, we can determine the following key pair:

- Public key (n = 3233, e = 17)
- Private key (n = 3233, d = 2753)

Now we can convert our secret message "BLOCKCHAIN" into numeric form by using an alphabet-based position substitution, yielding the numeric value. (We use a = 11, b = 12, etc., for simplicity.)

Making this substitution in the encryption process (i.e., $C = M^e \bmod(n)$), we obtain $C = 12^{17} \bmod (3233)$, yielding 1730, so the encrypted cipher text of the letter "B" is 1730.

To decrypt the ciphertext again, we use the decryption equation (i.e., $M = C^d \bmod(n)$) and substitute the private key values and the ciphertext (i.e., $M = 1730^{2753} \bmod (3233) = 12$).

7.4 Digital Signatures

7.4.1 Introduction

In the blockchain ecosystem, digital signatures are critical to enabling secure and authentic validations of transactions [4]. When any actor wants to transact on the blockchain (e.g., spend a digital currency token, validate the acceptance of a shipment), she must use the digital signature mechanism to validate the transition to the public.

Digital signatures, which are widely used and have broad applications that go beyond blockchains, range from the digital signing of documents to digital certificates and essentially all e-commerce transactions because digital signatures securely associate a signer with a document or message as part of a transaction. That is, the signatures ensure that the message originated from who claims to be the sender. Rather than the digital equivalent of an offline signature (e.g., stylus on tablet), digital signatures provide a mathematically verifiable method for authenticating a document; instead of a visual comparison of a pattern (i.e., the digital image of a signature), the authentication occurs via a secret key.

Electronic signatures are legally binding in twenty-seven countries, including China, the United States, Russia, Australia, Canada, and all countries in the European Union. The Anglo-Saxon countries, with their legal systems based on common law, have open, technology-neutral laws. In continental Europe, South America and Asia, multi-level models with defined standards based on digital signature technology have become established.

This section first outlines the motivation for digital signatures, especially in the blockchain realm. Then it reviews the technical mechanism for digital signatures based on RSA and walks through a concrete example and all of its calculations.

7.4.2 Motivation

We introduced the concepts of symmetric and asymmetric cryptography in Chap. 6 and Sect. 7.3, respectively. With the ability to communicate securely without having to pre-determine a shared key, one might think that all relevant security and communication requirements have been met. However, the blockchain use case has a key requirement that asymmetric encryption does not cover, which is the need for unambiguous message authentication.

Imagine a situation in which two communicating parties, Alice and Bob, want to use the Diffie-Helman key exchange to establish a shared secret key, k_s, so they can communicate securely.

In our example, Alice is a stockbroker and Bob is her client. Bob wants to buy 10,000 shares of Uber, so he sends this order to Alice, telling her to buy 10,000 Uber shares at the current price. Uber posts its earnings report throughout the day, and Bob realizes that the share price has gone down, so he claims that he never made an order, prompting Alice to sue Bob.

During the court hearing, Alice shows the judge Bob's order message as plaintext and in an encrypted format to prove that the message must have come from Bob. However, Bob argues that Alice generated this order herself, that he has no knowledge of it, and that because Alice was in possession of k_s, she could have created the order herself without Bob's knowledge. Based on the shared secret key alone, it is impossible for Alice to prove unambiguously that the order message came from Bob.

The solution to this problem, which comes from public-key cryptography, is elegant once the RSA principles are established: Digital signatures can be considered applications of the public key algorithm, so Bob can sign his order using his private key without revealing it, thus unambiguously establishing his identity in the transaction (i.e., via the ownership of the private key).

This process is fundamental for the enablement of blockchain operations: Any blockchain-based action (e.g., spending crypto coins, verifying identities, confirming orders) will be validated using digital signatures, so digital signatures provide a key tenet for enabling blockchain.

7.4.3 Usage

A digital signature is like a handwritten signature, only more secure. Since they require the sender (the signer) to have a pair of cryptographic keys—private key and a public key—digital signatures provide proof of message authenticity. Most important, digital signatures have the following attributes:

- Verification: Ability for Alice to prove that she is who she claims to be.
- Validation: Proof that the message was not tampered with during transmission.
- Non-repudiation: Inability for Alice to deny that she sent a message she signed.

The signing process involves a message to be signed locally by the sender (i.e., via private key) and the subsequent verification by the recipient (via the sender's public key). Figure 7.3. describes the steps of the signing process:

7.4.4 Signatures

We revisit the example from Sect. 7.5.2, where Bob wants to send a message to Alice, and Alice wants unambiguous proof of the message's origin. In this example, Bob has already created a public and private RSA key pair (Sect. 7.3.2):

- Public key (e, n)
- Private key (d, n)

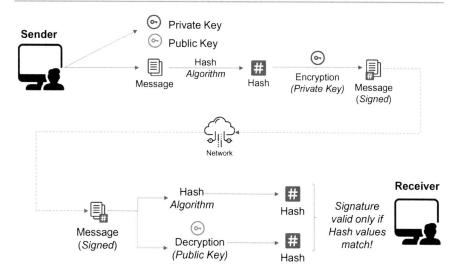

Fig. 7.3 Digital signature process

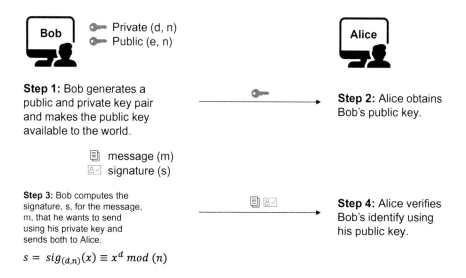

$$s = sig_{(d,n)}(x) \equiv x^d \ mod \ (n)$$

Fig. 7.4 Digital signature protocol

Based on his private key alone, Bob can create an unambiguous signature. In this process, the roles of the private and public keys are swapped such that, rather than the sender's using the public key for encryption, the sender uses the private key for authentication (Fig. 7.4).

Alice can verify the authenticity of the message, m, using Bob's public key. Following the set of equations established earlier, $x' \equiv s^e \bmod(n)$, so Alice knows that the signature is and only if $x' \equiv x \bmod(n)$. Because Bob is the only party who knows his private key, he can be unambiguously identified as the originator of the message.

We can show mathematically that this process will yield a valid statement only if the message has not been altered in transit. We begin based on the verification operation $s^e \bmod (n)$: $s^e = (x^d)^e = x^{d*e} = x \bmod(n)$. Based on the relationship between the public and private keys established in Sect. 7.3.2. (i.e., $d*e \bmod (m) = 1$), we know that raising an integer to the $(d*e)$th power modulo n will yield the integer again.

7.4.5   An Example

Bob wants to send a signed message ($x = 7$) to Alice. Just as in the regular RSA process, Bob creates a private key, derives a public key, and sends the public key to all recipients. However, unlike in asymmetric encryption, Bob uses his private key to sign the message that he wants to send to Alice. Alice then uses Bob's public key to validate the message's authenticity.

We use the same public and private keys as in our RSA example in Sect. 7.5.3:

- Public key (n = 3233, e = 17)
- Private key (n = 3233, d = 2753)

Next, Bob calculates the signature, s, for his message x (i.e., 7; the number 7 is just part of the message). Following the signature approach introduced in Sect. 7.5.3, Bob computes the signature for his message using the following formula:

$$s = x^d \bmod (n)$$
$$s = 7^{2753} \bmod (3233)$$
$$s = 7^{2753} \bmod (3233)$$
$$s = 2667$$

Based on this calculation, we know that the signature, s, for Bob's message x (i.e., 7) is 2667. Bob now sends both this message and his signature to Alice, who then validates Bob's signature using his public key:

$$x' \equiv s^e \bmod (n)$$
$$x' \equiv 2667^{17} \bmod (3233)$$
$$x' = 7$$

From this, Alice can unambiguously conclude (and prove) that Bob sent the message, x, and that the message was not altered during transmission.

7.5   Quantum Resistance

7.5.1   Introduction

Although quantum computing is only just now coming into the spotlight, concerns have already emerged that it will one day effortlessly undo the blockchain encryption layers, thus rendering data susceptible to manipulation and unwanted appropriation by bad actors. For example, to appropriate bitcoins, an attacker may use his victim's 256-bit public key to calculate the corresponding private key. As we have shown, this process would take roughly 0.65 quintillion years with a regular computer, but it might be completed in less than ten minutes with a quantum-computer-based algorithm.

We know that, as part of the Bitcoin blockchain, an unencrypted public key is sent along with every Bitcoin transaction and left unencrypted during the time (usually around ten minutes) it takes for the network to confirm the block. In theory, that would be enough time for a quantum-equipped attacker to derive the private key from a public key and control the corresponding account.

7.5.2   Mechanism

Transistors in conventional computers capture data in terms of 1-s and 0-s. Is it raining today? If it is, 1; if it is not, 0. Computing is essentially combinations of these calculations, and with enough transistors, almost anything can be computed.

With quantum computers, it is possible for the same input, called a qubit, to represent both 0 and 1 at the same time, a non-binary state known as "quantum superposition." This feature makes quantum computing exponentially more powerful when one is solving certain problem classes.

Currently, the best quantum computer is likely Google's Bristlecone quantum computer, which has 72 qubits, although estimates are that one would need several thousand qubits to break today's cryptographic algorithms. However, as Fig. 7.5. shows, the number of qubits in experimental computers is increasing.

The most fundamental building elements for Blockchain technology are digital signatures algorithms and cryptographic hashing algorithms, Shor's Algorithm and Grover's Algorithm, respectively. The quantum algorithms have put the security of these elements at risk.

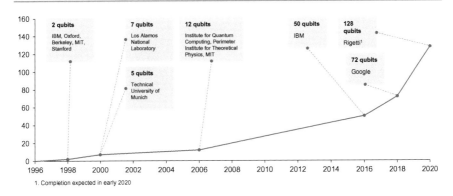

Fig. 7.5 Number of qubits achieved by date and organization

7.5.3 Shor's Algorithm

We have already discussed how asymmetric cryptography relies on the large prime numbers for public and private keys. The efficacy of this system hinges on current computers' practical inability to find the prime factors of these numbers.

Shor's (theoretical) algorithm is designed to find the prime factors by reducing the steps it takes to solve for a number's prime factors, thus threatening the integrity of public and private keys [5]. As an estimate, it would take a normal computer approximately 10^{39} operations to find the private key linked to a public key, while it would take a quantum algorithm 2,097,152 computations to determine the corresponding private key.

7.5.4 Grover's Algorithm

Although the cryptographic hash function could prove trickier for a full cryptographic computer to crack, Grover's Algorithm could be used to break cryptographic hashing algorithms by allowing users to search through an unordered list to find certain items [6]. Using quantum computing's super-position to calculate multiple inputs in one go, Grover's Algorithm could let users perform multiple rounds of calculations, where the probability of an item's containing a condition goes up each time. The algorithm narrows the list and produces the result with the highest probability of being correct. Using Grover's Algorithm on a regular computer would require 10^{78} operations to come up with the correct hash, while a quantum algorithm would require 10^{39} operations to crack the correct hash.

7.5.5 Imminence

Governmental and private organizations have been experimenting with quantum computing for applications in such areas as national defense, financial services, machine learning, and biomedical simulations. IBM expects to have an operational general-purpose quantum computer within a few years, while Google expects to achieve quantum supremacy, a quantum device capable of outperforming traditional computers, by the end of 2019. While no one is certain when quantum-computing technology will be advanced enough to crack a blockchain, some estimate it will occur within the next decade, with more conservative predictions putting it between twenty and thirty years.

7.5.6 Security Considerations

The blockchain community has already presented several solutions to the impending threat of quantum computing and appears confident that solutions will be in place by the time quantum computers become commonly available. Going beyond merely employing the most quantum-resistant cryptographic algorithms in the blockchain realm, developers envision an upgrade from the existing ECC-based encryption used in blockchain, and upgrades to quantum-based cryptography of just about every password-protected account available today.

7.5.7 Quantum Resistance

Until the wider academic community tests and accepts a quantum-resistant algorithm, there is no assurance that any of these blockchains will be sufficiently robust in the face of quantum computers. NIST tentatively expects drafts for standardization will be completed around 2022.

Developing the algorithm might not be the most difficult part for large blockchains like Ethereum and Bitcoin. Owners of centralized protocols can update the system as they please, but blockchains require broad consensus among many thousands of miners to pass an upgrade, as, if there is an upgrade, all wallets that are not yet quantum-resistant become vulnerable to attack, including the one million bitcoins mined by Bitcoin's pseudonymous inventor, Satoshi Nakamoto.

7.6 Exercise

7.6.1 Introduction

The exercise for this chapter require you to use both the RSA-based and the ECC-based public key methods. For each method, you will generate a public and a private key before validating the encryption and decryption functionality.

We include two methods to demonstrate the difference in the resulting key size, as RSA requires much larger keys to achieve the same level of encryption strength. This is why most modern applications have already switched to using ECC-based public-key cryptography schemes.

Again, for simplicity, we use the same docker-based approach of launching a plain Ubuntu instance for working through the exercise, just as we did in Chap. 6.

As before, use the following command in the Windows console to download and start an interactive version of Ubuntu:

```
docker run -i -t --name aes ubuntu
```

Following this entry, you will see the following set-up, which means that you are in the command-line environment of a simulated Unix environment and ready to start the blockchain experiments. (The string following "root@" will be different than from the example displayed below.)

```
root@<your-instance>:/#
```

7.6.2   Message Prep

First, create a simple text file containing the message that you want to encrypt. The content of the message in our example is shown below, but you can change the content of the text file to anything you like.

```
> echo "Attack at 5:00. RSA" > message.txt
```

Next, use the *cat* command to confirm that the contents of the message were stored correctly. (The output should simply be the message that you entered in the first step.)

```
> cat message.txt
Attack at 5:00. RSA
```

7.6.3   Key Generation (RSA)

Next, generate a private key. This key should never leave your computer or be sent to anyone; it is your private key and you should retain full control of it.

```
> openssl genpkey -algorithm RSA -out private.txt
.....................................................+++++
.............................................................+++++
```

Next, look at the private key that you have just generated using the *cat* command you have seen before:

```
> cat private.txt

-----BEGIN PRIVATE KEY-----
MIIEvgIBADANBgkqhkiG9w0BAQEFAASCBKgwggSkAgEAAoIBAQDi49avPKPz+2me
ZQQpjpOBjxCd337C2CVyRPdqaXQbbHvEQCE4OqgFCi13ZOQSBXsXDI7s2OUm3He6
37fKKJQmM44TvcwZT1vib6iyoQZ7MYFTiXIHVjjcWyMLa0SahXOImF0YigXEJz53
b23/XsdavUnjenpqBk6qqfst/EOg9pW9KcEfQQUtGr+8A3EKY7PTs7PApwju28uU
jJ4BQbyva+RX/GB6t6OsfnzCvhfs6ANidjuwcKWBaJ5umvd8xFwb9twyhBTbr2jj
riIseM9eD/m//Rm/uSlR3Hv4Cl69ESniT5k+3fCbFaC5LxMyvaPq6y9SZMRKDgUR
bS/kCUYZAgMBAAECggEAEhXnPwCucPxRZvbWZhmfWGx2/p6aFB32ni0xK6JMRwNW
ukYCX+ENE5nEFghMxcL6FNRDcE25tmdMg/DhTZP+ey0Q3jH62umggWQ1Jkf/pEJF
9Mq39C3DSo1ZNcfPKCILG5BJm3MlEoWuTQbs1bZQXcNI6IES0PC/xIrYIspA+cuH
pThybkLlcrxXyGm5qvN+5vvbCG4lf1JX5bQsNVFmJjIayLNc5VZQbsxXH1kkplf+
BRypUSuUCQFOvF7DebCngACUDT9GgwcLlIWdY3/csKbEF17jgena6ZjN1qlwlwtM
guZm0QJyeyjVcK3IE+5fNbIL3+abZU1DGgr1jwc0gQKBgQD21RiTVw0byNFVV8qq
2RstNK0/7B192hePtvQwCb+2xBBZmWk/2rlQnHTFc7RxeHyuB5gfQ1FJW3LfSKlT
wEr/JuVVIozUs5FVhp7l1gobUIuNK3IKr+jBl3Ox3bMj+ExiLKVqj6A/Z4uxUS+Z
lvcfbrje7UskJSFeSpcc6bhvXQKBgQDrUSDgnTWwqZbqWr0uPsBl9ewWUMFQZlFn
xXtTPDtJXpqcpAHMsd6tw7+5FpJGbk+tUCa2/rhkKAzjuLAtUaNAss93fMn7b/rc
TbYmVDcGWviga6AWeJ387MzJWFFiu4+uUMTBuif1iHLGj2+Peoc+5TNpyCnt987W
P0laOykR7QKBgQC6sSjaYHBAwJ5cX3+hw35DreEQRSV1SBykDawaHXWM5jS7oEY0
Dto1d3D223HylUAwXPwZQVBdHLcA3TN9bicLX777qps8Uekt+Bl9G2wfhsdWajLi
lHSG4GeYc2gIX8heRQiEVcfNzSKiZhaLo9ycQKHBs1cvKopXiDFNpBVk3QKBgBhn
wJ4rD99zp0hFAuvh7Dhm6gZid7or8nNtwt2eGJQCcMygIeOl6u9gpui+U4tkc3UJ
JArEnkEc+kE/7V214tWZ9FRxh81BDuZ8VNDi2RYap0CUCPVrqw8JTC/xrfcsdrlg
fReOhAhuD2FSjQJ3dcFrKgrljJu2oMgNpkDqc9b9AoGBAIkbU3K+1gmqrKoYeVj2
BPxReB2jOMv7SMbggtRImJ9qFLyI3mk5vnW84EsUPdT21788csVW28AdkGhHevFN
OU/v1BfGgJsVZvewrovNY6z2Mz04jfFTWUNxJ0xJSJpzItLQOwxuUZQBxElCKnlX
v7FBEZcOPXA9KmiKcbONJY11
-----END PRIVATE KEY-----
```

Now create the public key from the private key using the following command:

```
> openssl rsa -in private.txt -pubout > public.txt
writing RSA key
```

Again, using the *cat* command, you can display the public key after creating it. You will notice that the public key is much shorter than the private key:

```
> cat public.txt

-----BEGIN PUBLIC KEY-----
MIIBIjANBgkqhkiG9w0BAQEFAAOCAQ8AMIIBCgKCAQEA4uPWrzyj8/tpnmUEKY6T
gY8Qnd9+wtglckT3aml0G2x7xEAhODqoBQotd2TkEgV7FwyO7NjlJtx3ut+3yiiU
JjOOE73MGU9b4m+osqEGezGBU4lyB1Y43FsjC2tEmoVziJhdGIoFxCc+d29t/17H
Wr1J43p6agZOqqn7LfxDoPaVvSnBH0EFLRq/vANxCm0z07OzwKcI7tvLlIyeAUG8
r2vkV/xgerejrH58wr4X7OgDYnY7sHClgWiebpr3fMRcG/bcMoQU269o464iLHjP
Xg/5v/0Zv7kpUdx7+ApevREp4k+ZPt3wmxWguS8TMr2j6usvUmTESg4FEW0v5AlG
GQIDAQAB
-----END PUBLIC KEY-----
```

7.6.4   Digital Signatures (RSA)

We are finally ready to sign the message using SHA-256. Use the sign option of the OpenSSL package. The command will create a binary signature output file, signature.bin:

```
> openssl dgst -SHA256 -sign private.txt -out signature.bin message.txt
```

To be able to look at your signature output file, convert it into base64 format from its previous binary state using the following command:

```
> openssl base64 -in signature.bin -out signature.txt
```

Now you can see what the signature file looks like:

```
> cat signature.txt

B86Mrwp8ok0jgRolFvspFPJ9FRf716r89J1tBr80WTcyv0NWfhl35DDBxJv9gqCZ
BDY04kv6e+xIgzDibtuTFt7hYhKke7Bx9Z15rSsUyzXxP5L+qzwJ7Vo8+7sQfgVq
/ijcd2+zRkWpT4evxly/bC3eiQcuLvy6y3c2F4TXFHTa2nFQthCmtOQAj0H/YVJT
amhU8zh9M4o89TVJuQHaIO8t8Cvb9+fTlpddbXgerKicVM27pX2nqZIqU0UAZ9uE
xwY5kO5/qr6kM+FEbm8yCTOdJliP7Lo4FUPCZZ44D4BLwwpv4ucEs3H/9OLrr+D7
p88i17kG0QSvelxHqXG/TA==
```

Finally, validate that the signature is valid using the OpenSSL package, as well as the public.txt message file and the binary signature file (signature.bin). Notice that you do not need the private key for the validation process!

```
> openssl dgst -SHA256 -verify public.txt -signature signature.bin message.txt
Verified OK
```

7.6.5   Key Generation (Elliptic Curves)

For the ECC-based method, just as before, create a simple text file containing the message that you want to encrypt. The content of the message in our example is shown below, you can change the content of the text file to anything you like.

```
> echo "Attack at 5:00. ECC" > message.txt
```

Next, use the *cat* command to confirm that the contents of the message were stored correctly. (The output should be the message that you entered in the first step.)

```
> cat message.txt
Attack at 5:00. ECC
```

As you did with RSA, generate a private key for the ECC method. This key should never leave your computer or be sent to anyone; it is your private key and you should retain full control of it.

```
> openssl ecparam -genkey -name prime256v1 -out private.txt
```

Using the *cat* command, look again at the private key for ECC that you just generated. You will notice that this key is much shorter than the key that you generated via the RSA method:

```
> cat private.txt

-----BEGIN EC PARAMETERS-----
Bg_gqhkjOPQMBBw==
-----END EC PARAMETERS-----
-----BEGIN EC PRIVATE KEY-----
MHcCAQEEII3RXDIHnvz7a1KJ5FeuRGgpKUliFy2uYExSsqjJF9V7oAoGCCqGSM49
AwEHoUQDQgAEjRC6Wo8vrKjHxvEYur/fr4Dnd9vzkIgBbHKUW2SXo6gMJOE2xewr
sCXeNzgSAiJD5D6FaFBiopbTGzRVXZ7ScA==
-----END EC PRIVATE KEY-----
```

Next, create the ECC public key from the private key that you just generated:

```
> openssl ec -in private.txt -pubout -out public.txt
read EC key
writing EC key
```

Again, use the *cat* command to look at what the public key looks like:

```
> cat public.txt

-----BEGIN PUBLIC KEY-----
MFkwEwYHKoZIzj0CAQYIKoZIzj0DAQcDQgAEjRC6Wo8vrKjHxvEYur/fr4Dnd9vz
kIgBbHKUW2SXo6gMJOE2xewrsCXeNzgSAiJD5D6FaFBiopbTGzRVXZ7ScA==
-----END PUBLIC KEY-----
```

7.6.6 Digital Signatures (Elliptic Curves)

For ECC, you will again use the -sign option of the OpenSSL package. The command shown below will create a binary signature output file, signature.bin:

```
> openssl dgst -SHA256 -sign private.txt -out signature.bin message.txt
```

As before, to see your signature output file, convert it into base64 format from its previous binary state using the following command:

```
> openssl base64 -in signature.bin -out signature.txt
```

Now you can see what the signature file looks like:

```
> cat signature.txt
MEQCIB0jy8YvwHfKWHzAibc5pfadv7yAWQduO4h3JRDpxXkHAiBLWar/Kt2Js106
iVuYcgvkAEnQn1W+v3vAeNlxMm8eZg==
```

Finally, you can validate that the signature is valid using the OpenSSL package, as well as the public.txt message file and the binary signature file (signature.bin). Notice that you do not need the private key for the validation process!

```
> openssl dgst -SHA256 -verify public.txt -signature signature.bin message.txt
Verified OK
```

References

1. Rivest R, Shamir A, Adleman L (1978) A method for obtaining digital signatures and public-key cryptosystems. https://people.csail.mit.edu/rivest/Rsapaper.pdf
2. Barker E, Chen L, Roginsky A et al (2018) Recommendation for pair-wise key-establishment schemes using discrete logarithm cryptography. https://doi.org/10.6028/NIST.SP.800-56Ar3
3. OpenSSL. https://www.openssl.org/docs/man1.1.1/man1/openssl.html
4. The Keyed-Hash Message Authentication Code (HMAC) (2008). https://nvlpubs.nist.gov/nistpubs/FIPS/NIST.FIPS.198-1.pdf
5. Cavanaugh J (2017) Probabilistic and statistical methods in cryptology. Springer Nature, Jersey City
6. Portugal R (2013) Quantum walks and search algorithms. Springer, New York

Part III
Real-World Applications

Blockchain in Action: Real-World Applications

8

8.1 Introduction

Now that we are nearing the end of our exploration of the workings and details of blockchain, it would be worthwhile to overview instances in which this technology has lent itself well to execution and been applied to advantage. As is often the case with potentially disruptive innovations, adoption proceeds slowly as actors learn about the technology and how best to harness its potential. Blockchain solutions have yet to reach the mass market, but there are promising signs—not least from the technology industry's leaders—that a new phase in the adoption cycle is on the horizon. For example, in June 2019, Facebook published its Libra White Paper [1], announcing its intention to launch its own cryptocurrency by the same name. Hearings have already been held in the US Congress, with many lawmakers questioning Facebook's motives and the nature of the project itself: The prospect of a global, decentralized currency uncontrolled by any government agency is both exciting and daunting.

While Libra has the potential to be the most consequential example of a real-world application of blockchain technology, there are several others. This final chapter offers a selection of the most noteworthy implementations of blockchain and surveys a wide range of seemingly disparate fields where production systems have been created. To that end, the chapter delves into real-world examples sampled from the following topics, while highlighting their successes, failures, and outlooks:

- Currencies (e.g., Facebook Libra)
- Cross-border Transfers (e.g., Ripple)
- Tokenization (e.g., Everledger)
- Asset Tracking (e.g., Provenance)
- Commodity Trading (e.g., Omega Grid)

© Springer Nature Switzerland AG 2020
D. Hellwig et al., *Build Your Own Blockchain*, Management for Professionals,
https://doi.org/10.1007/978-3-030-40142-9_8

8.2   Currencies

Over the course of this book, we have come to know cryptocurrencies as the most prominent current application of the blockchain technology. Bitcoin is the most famous among these digital currencies, and while it is still not quite a mass phenomenon, its speculative nature has attracted intense public scrutiny and awareness. Bitcoin has also significantly contributed to popularizing blockchain as a concept.

The idea of having a global, blockchain-based currency was propelled to the forefront with Facebook's announcement of Libra. While Libra does not differ fundamentally from most other cryptocurrencies, its sheer ambition raises the prospect of a global currency for everyday transactions, one that is governed by distributed consensus rather than any central (i.e., governmental) authority. The core problem Facebook professes it aims to solve with Libra is the lack of access to the financial system by the 1.7 billion people around the world who are currently unable to benefit from it, as well as lower-income households' paying a disproportionate amount of their modest budgets for services like wire-transfer fees, ATM charges, and overdrafts. Facebook's aspiration is, as stated in the Libra White Paper, "to deliver on the promise of the 'internet of money.' " Accessible by anyone from anywhere, it is essentially a global alternative to the traditional financial infrastructure that leaves out or takes unfair advantage of too many people [1].

While Facebook's venture builds on the expertise and experiences of existing cryptocurrencies, its ambitions are greater in scope, so Facebook is building its own system from the ground up. A major problem with digital currencies that Facebook seeks to address is a lack of stability: Since these currencies, including Bitcoin and Ether, are not backed by underlying assets, their value tends to fluctuate wildly, which makes them attractive to speculators and investors but prevents their widespread adoption:

> Just as consumers in Europe know the number of Euros it takes them to buy a coffee today will be similar to the number of Euros it will take them tomorrow, holders of Libra, too, can be confident the value of their coins today will be relatively stable across time. [1]

Hence, a key feature of Libra that differentiates it from most major competitors is the Libra Reserve, a basket of low-risk liquid assets consisting of bank deposits and short-term government-issued securities that back every Libra Coin created. The goal of the reserve is value preservation, which will engender trust in the currency's stability, making it a "stablecoin." The concept of stablecoins is not new, but despite their promise to take cryptocurrencies mainstream, they represent only a small fraction of the crypto realm and are rarely used for payments [2]. The funds for the Libra Reserve will come from Founding Members, who invest in a separate Investment Token, and from the users of Libra. For every new Libra coin created, an equivalent amount of fiat money will have to be paid to the Reserve. Therefore, as the demand for Libra grows, so will its Reserve.

Another unique element of Libra is the Libra Association, an independent body that governs the ecosystem. While Facebook is initially assuming a position of primus inter pares, when its launches, it will transition to becoming an equal stakeholder in Libra. The list of participants in the Association (i.e., the Founding Members) shows the possibly unprecedented scale of the project, despite some recent regulation-induced withdrawals (e.g., Visa, Mastercard).

The Libra ecosystem will be built around the Libra blockchain, which will be implemented by a new open-source software called Move.

A likely point of contention is that, for the time being, only Association members can become validator nodes, making Libra a permissioned blockchain. (See Sect. 1.6.1.) Facebook claims it will begin the transition to a permissionless system within five years of launch.

8.3 Cross-Border Transfers

Cross-border payments are another area in which blockchain technology has been applied with notable early success. A battle is already being fought over the future of this multi-billion-dollar market and it is unfolding as a Silicon Valley cliché: from its palatial headquarters outside Brussels, SWIFT, a traditional interbank messaging service established half a century ago, dominates the market with its network of approximately 11,000 financial institutions around the world. Aiming to "replace SWIFT" (in the words of CEO Brad Garlinghouse) is Ripple Labs, a San Francisco startup founded in 2012 that is developing the Ripple payment protocol based on distributed ledger technology with the goal of streamlining cross-border transfers. Despite commanding only a fraction of SWIFT's market share, Ripple is already challenging the status quo.

Compared to domestic payments, innovation has long lagged in the arena of international payments, even though revenue per transaction is significantly higher, estimated at $45 per cross-border payment by a recent McKinsey *Global Payments* report, with total global revenue exceeding $200 billion [3]. Traditionally, when a customer makes a payment to an account in another country, a chain of banks moves the payment message until it reaches the intended recipient, a process requiring two or more days (Table 8.1). This system of corresponding banks is necessary if the sending bank (e.g., in Norway) has no established relationship with the receiving bank (e.g., in the Philippines). Until recently, this process was slow, non-transparent, costly, and beset with errors. Payments often took several days to reach their destinations, not least because of required intervention by bank clerks, confirmation of payment completion was hard to come by, and banks often deducted fees without the customers' prior knowledge.

Ripple stepped into this scenario with its xCurrent real-time gross settlement system, which enables cross-border payments within a matter of seconds using blockchain technology and real-time messaging. The fintech, which also runs XRP (the third-largest cryptocurrency, behind only Bitcoin and Ether), signed up

Table 8.1 Comparison of methods for international transfers

	Hashing	Symmetric	Asymmetric
Architecture	Centralized	Decentralized	Decentralized
Settlement	Clearing and settlement	Proof of work	Consensus
Speed	2 + business days	10–60 minute	3–6 s
Peak volume	19 million messages/day	600,000 transactions/day	86 million messages/day
Currency	FIAT	BTC	Universal
Transaction cost	Operator fees	Mining fees	Security fees

heavyweights from the financial sector like American Express, Brazilian Itaú Unibanco, Banco Santander, and Standard Chartered. Most of Ripple's major partners have so far chosen to use xCurrent without relying on XRP as their currency to settle payments, as the cryptocurrency is considered too volatile compared to fiat currency. There are signs that this preference could change, as banks around the world have taken note of the proliferation of stablecoins and with future projects aiming to raise the standing of cryptocurrencies. More consequentially, Ripple has just bought a 10% stake in MoneyGram, the world's second-largest remittance company. MoneyGram has agreed to use Ripple's newest product, xRapid, which relies on XRP to settle payments.

Whether Ripple and blockchain technology will come to dominate the cross-border payments market remains to be seen. Banks are uneasy about the degree of transparency offered by blockchain (i.e., one of the technology's key features). Indeed, financial institutions are reluctant to let their competitors investigate their books. What is clear is that the start-up has caused a "ripple" in an industry that has run on the same model for forty-five years.

The massive bank-owned conglomerate SWIFT felt sufficiently threatened by the upstart Ripple, along with various other ventures, that it began to innovate heavily: in 2017, SWIFT launched a new service called SWIFT gpi, which provides same-day cross-border payments, end-to-end tracking, and greater transparency [4]. The company also began experimenting with blockchain technology, but has, for the moment at least, dismissed it as overly complex and as failing to address the deeper challenges of cross-border payments. Nonetheless, SWIFT has partnered with R3, a DLT technology company, and recently announced that it has settled cross-border payments within seconds in a worldwide trial.

8.4 Tokenization

As introduced in Chap. 1, tokenization describes the process of converting rights to an asset into digital tokens. Consider an asset, a sports car that is worth $100,000. Tokenization can digitally represent and transform this sports car into 100,000 tokens. (The number is arbitrary; we could have picked 2 million or 200,000 tokens instead.) Each token represents a 0.001% share of the underlying asset. The tokens are subsequently issued on a platform that supports smart contracts (e.g., Ethereum), allowing the tokens to be traded on various exchanges. By buying one token, a person buys a 0.001% ownership stake in the underlying asset; buying 50,000 tokens results in half ownership of the assets.

One area that already leverages blockchain-enabled tokenization is the art industry. Art transactions today are complex and often delicate transactions. Both buyers and sellers may want to remain anonymous for various reasons, and a buyer's funds are difficult to validate a priori. In addition, ownership of valuable artwork is a delicate topic (e.g., artworks have potentially questionable origins, and/or owners may not want their ownership of the art to be public information). This field could benefit from blockchain, especially if this nascent technology can guarantee secure and transparent purchases of art.

Previous ventures into the digital world by established auction houses have largely been marked by failure, but, the art market is now gradually attempting to benefit from blockchain. Consider the sale of the Barney A. Ebsworth Collection in November 2018 by Christie's of New York: Prior to attending the auction event, potential buyers could access the blockchain-based system to view the provenance and transaction histories of all the works on offer.

Especially relevant to the art market is that blockchain makes transactions more transparent. For example, the auction house can use blockchain to validate whether a buyer has the funds required. Furthermore, the entire transaction sequence, including the ownership transfer, can, in theory, be executed via a smart contract. Smart contracts can be used to determine whether the seller really owns the artwork, as the digital contract cannot be altered, and the chain of sales transactions that have taken place can be verified. Furthermore, the contracts are accessible to all, thus facilitating the traceability of provenances. Finally, blockchain also gives artists the opportunity to prove that they are the true creators of their work, thereby curtailing incidents of counterfeit.

However, the increased transparency of transactions also entails the loss of anonymity, a feature prized by the art market. Therefore, the extent to which this technology will be incorporated into the art market will depend on whether the market can comply with ever-stricter money-laundering regulations while granting the degree of anonymity those who transact in artworks demand.

8.5 Asset Tracking

Traceability of provenances can also be applied to goods other than those in the art industry, such as commodities. Consider the SBMP project, an initiative run by the Queensland Cane Growers Association that aims to improve the traceability of sugar products from farms to factories to suppliers to retailers.

Using blockchain, the agency's goal is to ensure that Australia's sugar supply is traceable and understandable, thereby enabling consumers to know where their sugar comes from and allowing Australian sugar products to be distinguished from other imports. Here, a blockchain-enabled system protects a database against tampering by unscrupulous parties who are likely to benefit from a lack of consumer inventions and lack of transparency. Blockchain also allows the Australian sugar industry to track the market's reaction to imported sugar with an eye to beating competitors. Finally, retail consumers can use the blockchain to track the individual codes of products (e.g., sugar packets) so they know exactly when the sugar was made, where it came from, and other relevant data (e.g., fair-trade certificates).

While experts expect blockchain to increase the cost of producing sugar by virtue of its being a value-adding project, the Queensland government and farmers predict that the difference will be offset by the expected increase in demand. In fact, policymakers are predicting an increase in demand as soon as the blockchain becomes operational.

8.6 Commodity Trading

Blockchain technology has the potential to become the dominant design backbone for public energy's charging and billing transactions (e.g., for electric vehicles). Nevertheless, the potential for blockchain-mediated cost reductions in the energy market is limited. Especially in markets where digital solutions have already proven their worth, blockchain technology will meet strong competitive products and services that are already in use.

Blockchain's potential in emerging markets may be significantly greater than its currently realized potential. As a decentralized digital platform that enables secure data storage and transactions in peer-to-peer networks for the energy market

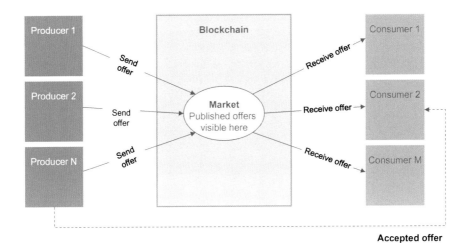

Fig. 8.1 Blockchain-enabled energy market (illustrative)

in emerging economies, blockchain technology can make intermediary instances (e.g., banks) redundant by enabling transactions to occur directly between energy producers and consumers (Fig. 8.1).

The use of blockchain in the energy sector could simplify the integration of numerous decentralized generation facilities and promote the use of renewable energies. This development may lead to new digital business models in the energy industry, allowing energy providers to develop applications and systems that will lead to new license- and fee-based revenue streams for these providers. However, such an endeavor could require considerable convincing to propel the providers to abandon the status quo and to experiment with the implementation of new technologies.

8.7   Looking Ahead

8.7.1   Humble Beginnings

Bitcoin received little public attention when it was introduced in early 2009. It took more than a year after Satoshi Nakamoto mined the first Bitcoin block on January 3 of the same year for the first real-world Bitcoin transaction to occur: On May 18, 2010, Laszlo Hanyecz offered 10,000 bitcoins for the delivery of two Domino's pizzas (Fig. 8.2). It took four days, until May 22, 2010, for someone to agree to the transaction. As of September 2019, these 10,000 bitcoins are worth a little over 100 million dollars [5].

As the Bitcoin project was being launched in 2008/2009, the latest world financial crisis was approaching its peak. The entire world was focused on the faltering financial markets, and the spectacular experiment of a decentralized, non-state-controlled, and universally accessible digital currency was largely ignored by speculators everywhere.

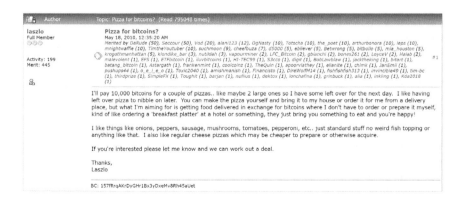

Fig. 8.2 Request for the first real-world Bitcoin transaction

For a few years after their initial launch, both the Bitcoin cryptocurrencies and the associated blockchain technology were still considered hype. Despite a continued surge in the price of bitcoins, the public's perception of Bitcoin as a controversial currency was unchanged, exacerbated by the myriad examples of Bitcoin's illicit uses (e.g., for pseudo-anonymous darknet marketplaces). Redeeming the reputations of both cryptocurrencies and blockchain has taken years, a process that is ongoing, and many today still cannot tell the two apart.

However, times appear to be changing. In a 2018 report, the World Economic Forum predicted that by 2025 roughly 10 percent of global gross domestic product (GDP) will be processed using blockchain, perhaps an unsurprising outcome considering the vast realm of applications that are enabled by blockchain technology, which go far beyond cryptocurrencies. Indeed, fueled by the introduction and availability of smart contracts, we are increasingly moving away from a myriad of cryptocurrency applications and implementations, such as Bitcoin, Ethereum, and Libra, to a much broader set of applications. Blockchain-based implementations have not only leveraged the new technology and privacy components that are specific to the technology's underlying structure but have also fueled discussions around the establishment of common standards to drive simplification (e.g., within the logistics and financial space). Even in fields that are not directly related to blockchain's core capability of safe record-keeping, employing blockchain-related approaches has allowed of problems to be tackled that have so far seemed intractable (e.g., the implementation of a working model for decentralized trading of carbon credits).

8.7.2 A Word of Caution

As with all new technologies, blockchain-enabled solutions should be approached with caution. In many instances, the prevalent and indiscriminate roll-out of blockchain-enabled solutions appears to be driven by the rationale that, because the cryptocurrency use-case worked well, other general problems (e.g., financial services, transaction monitoring) should be easily addressable using the same means and approaches. However, applying a solution that was meant to solve one problem (e.g., cryptocurrencies), to solve other problems is equivalent to saying that, because there is only a hammer, everything must look and work like a nail. Furthermore, applications of distributed ledger technologies (DLT) are not seamless: DLT-based projects often spend more time setting up governance and working groups than solving real-world problems (e.g., tracking of humanitarian aid, selective information sharing).

Therefore, one must exercise caution when planning blockchain-based applications and consider potentially unintended consequences, such as data privacy implications, and acknowledge that blockchain is not likely a silver bullet for *all* problems. In the end, blockchains are just another tool or, more accurately, the underlying plumbing in a generalized approach to find solutions to an eclectic set of problems. Indeed, blockchains in their various flavors provide a protocol-like approach to enabling decentralized trust.

8.7.3 The Jury Is Still Out

There is much to look forward to in the blockchain realm: The field of distributed ledger technology is rife with opportunity at all levels, including network and database theory, mathematical and cryptographical models, and industry-specific implementations. The confluence of these fields and their applications is something to watch out for, with the next decade being likely to bring about exciting new opportunities.

Many today consider blockchain-enabled innovation, especially cryptocurrencies, a Ponzi scheme that has no real underlying value. This understandable suspicion bears many similarities to that shown to the internet industry in its early days. The business model of the internet industry from 1995 to 2000 was to drive IPOs and raise stock prices through savvy marketing. With the dot-com bubble's bursting in the early 2000s, considerable market value was destroyed. However, we all benefit today from the innovation that this destruction engendered. Most of the core technologies and developer knowledge we use today was funded out of the dot-com venture, and after the most stock-price-focused companies disappeared in the early 2000s, internet businesses that focused on solving tangible problems were finally able to do so. Indeed, most of the truly revolutionary internet companies were started around or shortly before this time, many of which remain highly relevant today (e.g., Amazon, eBay, Google, PayPal).

There is little question that blockchain-enabled models will be employed to solve myriad problems around the world and in many industries. These solutions and applications will not all come as easily or as rapidly as people may expect and may initially be met with skepticism, but there are plenty of examples of businesses with problems that can be solved using blockchain technology, and they are willing to listen. In May of 2019, the state of Rhode Island issued a broad RFP to explore the viability of blockchain technology to improve state operations. Just weeks after the RFP announcement, Germany issued a position paper calling for blockchain to be used for the country's public service tasks, administrative services, electronic health records, document protection, and company registrations. This trend is likely to continue. Following an initial wave of hype that focused primarily on the financial services industry, less-obvious actors are starting to explore the potential of blockchain technology for their realms (e.g., government operations and services). As understanding of the technology continues to broaden, additional capabilities (e.g., selective information-sharing) will lead to the discovery of additional use cases, as well as, finally, the realization of tangible value.

This likely sequence of events is similar to the time of the dot-com bubble. In retrospect, there were only a few entrepreneurs, such as Jeff Bezos and Peter Thiel and Elon Musk, who could be considered technology pioneers. They built Apache, Mozilla, Linux, and MySQL during the dot-com days. Similarly, credit is owed to the engineers that continued to improve and scale the underlying technology infrastructure that enables most of our internet-centric applications today. We suspect that we will see the crystallization of a similar group of blockchain innovators as crypto IPOs play a more minor role. Indeed, when looking for the next

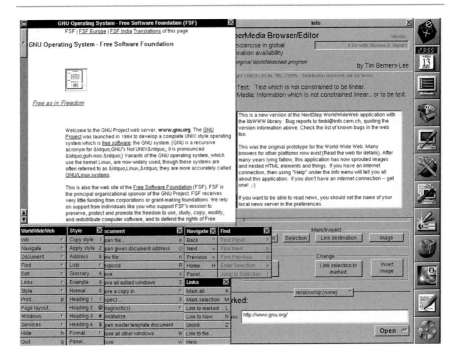

Fig. 8.3 First web browser released for the NeXT computer in 1990

silver bullet in the blockchain realm, we should seek out engineers who work tirelessly at building the infrastructure and developing the tools to scale blockchain-based solutions to solve large-scale tangible problems. Such solutions are likely to remain with us for decades to come.

Blockchain is driving a groundbreaking paradigm shift in value transfer, as the Internet has for information transfer. However, if this transformation is to have its full impact, the confluence of many areas of expertise, as well as commitment from key stakeholders in both the private and public sectors, will be required. Today's internet infrastructure is based on the so-called TCP/IP protocol. Initial multi-party tests of this protocol were conducted in 1977 between the US (Stanford University), the UK (University College London), and Norway, but it took another thirteen years for the "killer" application to be invented for the TCP/IP protocol—the first rudimentary web browser: the so-called WorldWideWeb [6], a browser developed in 1990 by Tim Berners-Lee for the NeXT Computer. (See Fig. 8.3.) Blockchain was invented in 2009, so if this timeline is a rubric, we'll have to wait a few more years to witness the crystallization of blockchain's "killer" application.

References

1. The Libra Association. An introduction to libra. https://libra.org/en-us/whitepaper
2. Furlonger D, Uzureau C (2019) The real business of blockchain: how leaders can create value in a new digital age. Harvard Business Review Press, Boston
3. Bansal S, Bruno P, Denecker O, Goparaju M, Niederkorn M (2018) Global payments 2018: a dynamic industry continues to break new ground. McKinsey & Company, New York
4. Loader D (2014) Clearing, settlement and custody. Elsevier, Amsterdam
5. Popper N (2016) Digital gold: bitcoin and the inside story of the misfits and millionaires trying to reinvent money. HarperCollins, New York
6. Berners-Lee T (2000) Weaving the web: the past present and future of the world wide web by its inventor. Texere, London

Index

© Springer Nature Switzerland AG 2020
D. Hellwig et al., *Build Your Own Blockchain*, Management for Professionals,
https://doi.org/10.1007/978-3-030-40142-9